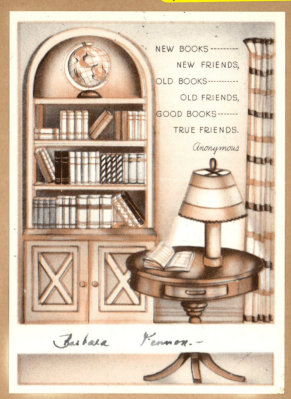

NEW BOOKS ---------
NEW FRIENDS,
OLD BOOKS ----------
OLD FRIENDS,
GOOD BOOKS -------
TRUE FRIENDS.

*Anonymous*

Barbara Kennon.

PUBLISHED BY ADAM AND CHARLES BLACK
SOHO SQUARE, LONDON, W.

AGENTS

AMERICA . . . THE MACMILLAN COMPANY
64 & 66 FIFTH AVENUE, NEW YORK

AUSTRALASIA . OXFORD UNIVERSITY PRESS
205 FLINDERS LANE, MELBOURNE

CANADA . . . THE MACMILLAN COMPANY OF CANADA, LTD.
27 RICHMOND STREET WEST, TORONTO

INDIA . . . . MACMILLAN & COMPANY, LTD.
MACMILLAN BUILDING, BOMBAY
309 BOW BAZAAR STREET, CALCUTTA

S. T. Hallston
Sydney N. S. W.

"PADDLING GENTLY OVER THE STILL WATERS"    *Page 33*

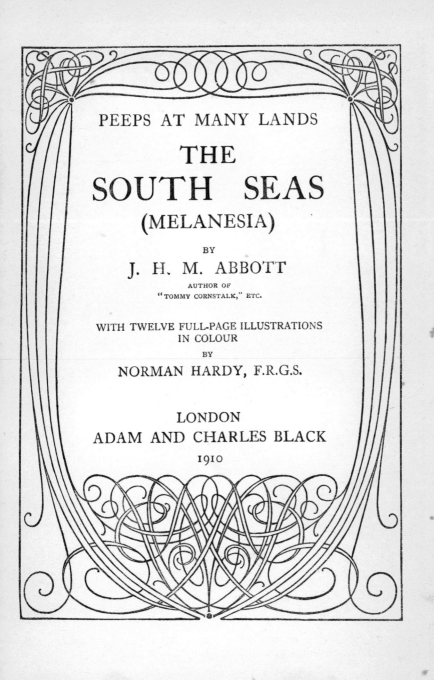

PEEPS AT MANY LANDS

# THE
# SOUTH SEAS
## (MELANESIA)

BY

## J. H. M. ABBOTT

AUTHOR OF
"TOMMY CORNSTALK," ETC.

WITH TWELVE FULL-PAGE ILLUSTRATIONS
IN COLOUR

BY

## NORMAN HARDY, F.R.G.S.

## LONDON
## ADAM AND CHARLES BLACK
1910

The Author wishes to acknowledge the assistance he has derived from the Rev. Dr. Codrington's "Melanesia" (Oxford: The Clarendon Press) and the "Solomon Islands" of the late Dr. H. B. Guppy, R.N. (London: Swan Sonnenschein), in the making of this little book. He would refer the reader who desires to make the fullest acquaintance possible of Melanesia, without going there, to these two fine works, together with "The Savage South Seas" of Messrs. Hardy and Elkington (London: A. and C. Black).

*First published September,* 1908

# CONTENTS

# LIST OF ILLUSTRATIONS

IN COLOUR

## By NORMAN HARDY, F.R.G.S.

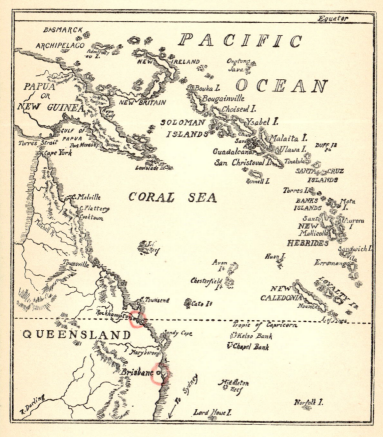

SKETCH-MAP OF MELANESIA.

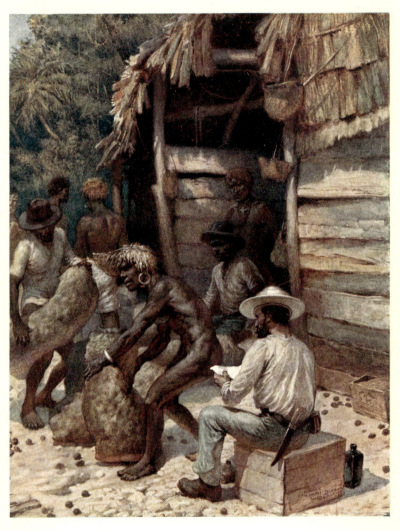

A SOUTH SEA ISLAND TRADER AND
HIS SACKS OF IVORY NUTS      *Page 52*

# THE SOUTH SEAS

## MELANESIA

### CHAPTER I

#### THE BLACK ISLANDS

A LONG way away from England and Europe, far away from civilization and the present day—almost, as it were, in the times of Mr. Punch's " Prehistoric Peeps "—lie The Black Islands. Geographically they are labelled Melanesia, but if you know any Greek—and perhaps, like the author, you don't—you will understand that that designation and Black Islands amount to pretty much the same thing. But you will not understand so readily, perhaps, why they are The Black Islands.

You must take a map—Mercator's Projection for preference —and see for yourself. On the right-hand side, low down below Asia, you will find Australia, and on the other side— which, curiously enough, is still the right-hand side (only you wouldn't think so)—are the two vast American continents. Between Australia and the western coast-line of the Americas lies an enormous space of Ocean, dotted, as you will see, with an infinity of islands and groups of islands. This great space comprises, roughly, that part of the world known as the South Sea Islands. And the South Sea Islands have been

# The South Seas

divided up, also rather roughly, into two great divisions called Polynesia (Many Islands) and Melanesia.*

However you take it, an island is an island—that is to say, a certain amount of rock and dirt completely surrounded by water—and although the islands of the South Seas often differ very greatly in geological formation and shape—from the ring of palm-grown coral, and the solitary volcano, to vast mountain ranges that tower up into the skies and stretch for hundreds of miles—they are all equally brilliant and splendid in their luxuriant tropical foliage, opal-tinted waters, and many-coloured gorgeousnesses of flower and bird. So that, so far as the actual appearance of the islands themselves goes, there seems to be no ground whatever for dubbing one division of them " Black."

But it is because of the differences in the races of people which inhabit them that the distinction has been made—possibly, also, because of the different characteristics of the people. In Melanesia—the islands on the Australian side, close to New Guinea, and below the Malay Peninsula and Archipelago—the native races are darker in colour than those which populate the islands of Polynesia away to the east, and towards the American coast. The Polynesians are generally handsome people, with straight hair, and complexions nearly resembling those of the Japanese. The Melanesians are, according to European ideas, at any rate, not remarkable for beauty of countenance, and their hair is frizzy and woolly, after the type of the negro race. The Polynesians have features almost as straight as those of good-looking English people, generally well-shaped mouths, and laughing eyes. The Melanesians have flat, wide, pug noses, thick lips, high cheek-bones, and some almost indescribable glint of savagery and barbarism in their eyes, which is hardly characteristic of the gentler and merrier Polynesian. So there you have

* There is also Micronesia, the Little Islands, with which we have nothing to do.

2

# The Black Islands

the difference between East and West in the South Pacific, and the reasons why the more westerly islands have been called " Black "—mainly because of the colour of the people who live in them, and, one cannot help fancying, a little because of their blacker and uglier moral attributes.

It is not, indeed, that one would wish to compare the Melanesian too unfavourably with the man of the Eastern Pacific. He has his bad points—and some of them are very, very bad—but he is not without his good ones. The Polynesian is, on the whole, the pleasanter fellow of the two, and a good deal more of a gentleman, but, "if it came to a row," one rather fancies that a number of well-led Westerners from certain " fighting " islands in Melanesia would be more than a match for an equal number of Polynesians just as well led. The Melanesian has had a harder life-history than the Polynesian. His struggle for existence has been more severe, his existence more precarious, and his chances fewer than those of the latter. If you take him all in all—his good points thrown in with his bad, his hardihood and courage mixed with his weaknesses and his superstitions, his virtues with his vices—you will not find him to be very much, if at all, the inferior of the Polynesian, though it is more than likely that you would prefer both the aspect and the society of the last-named to his. It is difficult indeed to compare the two races. Differences are often so slight and subtle as hardly to suggest themselves as such, and sometimes one is inclined to suspect that they are found where they do not really exist. There is a relationship indicated by certain words, and roots of words, and meanings of words, all through the Islands—a similarity of weapons, and tools of handicraft, and tribal customs that seems to argue a far back and long-forgotten common origin. But, on the other hand, there are so many real and great differences that it is easy to understand how The Black Islands vary from the rest, and have come to be labelled as different. It is to The Black Islands that we are bound, and now that we have

1—2

gone into the reason for their being so named, we will leave the prettier Polynesian alone. We shall find a few of them employed on plantations in Melanesia, and in the crews of trading schooners, but we shall be many hundreds of miles from their part of the Pacific.

If you turn to the map again—this time to the one a few pages back—you will see the extent of Melanesia. Broadly speaking, you may say that it begins to the South somewhere about the Tropic of Capricorn, and extends northward to the Equator. It is difficult to lay down any hard-and-fast lines as to its most easterly limits, but it certainly does not go beyond the Fiji Islands. Politically, indeed, Fiji is part and parcel of it—for there is installed the Government of the Western Pacific, in the person of the High Commissioner and his Secretaries, Assistants, Deputy-Assistants, and all the other personalities of Colonial Office rule. But the Fijians are not quite like the Melanesians proper. They would seem to be, rather, a link between East and West which possess the characteristics of both. Keeping an average distance from the curving coast-line of Australia, Melanesia bends north and north-west from New Caledonia and the Loyalty Islands, through the New Hebrides, Banks, and Santa Cruz groups to the Solomons, and then up round New Guinea, through New Britain and New Ireland, to the Bismarck Archipelago. Racially, New Guinea belongs to Melanesia, but it is such a vast continent of an island that there will not be room for it in this book. We will confine our voyagings from New Caledonia to the western end of the Solomons. For all practical purposes the islands through which we shall sail constitute Melanesia. And even then, though we shall have taken many months over our explorations, we shall have left hundreds, if not thousands, of islands unvisited. But we shall have seen enough to let us know what Melanesia is like, and to have taught us a little—a very little—concerning its strange people and their strange ways.

# The Black Islands

When you are looking at the maps of these islands there is always one thing to be remembered, and a very important thing, too. They are not as little as they look. What appears to you as something approaching Euclid's definition of a point may have a coast-line of ten to twenty miles, bays and harbours, running streams, and hills and mountains of no mean altitude. Though even the larger islands of the Solomons do not appear very large, it is worth while to remember that some of them contain a greater area of land than the largest of the English counties. The British Solomon Islands Protectorate is just about 1,000 miles from end to end, and there are more than 200,000 people living in it. It is well to remember that you do not proceed across most of these fly-specks in anything like a hop, step, and a jump— even if the wily " man belong bush " grant you a safe-conduct, which he never does.

## CHAPTER II

### OUT OF SYDNEY

THE highways that lead to Melanesia—the main world-roads— pass through three gateways, which do not lie very far apart. They are, so to speak, the " jumping-off " places for The Black Islands. You *may* go by other tracks—say, for instance, from San Francisco, or Vancouver, or even from the Albert Docks by way of Cape Horn—but these are such long jumps that nobody ever essays them. To be sure, the first white men went from Lima in Peru, but that was more than 300 years ago, and easier routes than that of Don Alvaro de Mendana and his stout navigator, Hernando Gallego, have since been opened up.

Sydney in New South Wales, Brisbane in Queensland, and

# The South Seas

Auckland in the North Island of New Zealand are the gateways. Of these Brisbane is the nearest,, Auckland a little nearer than Sydney, but Sydney the most notable and important. Whichever of the other gates you were to choose to enter Melanesia by—that is, assuming that you came from England—you would most probably pass through Sydney to reach it, and from Sydney you would find the best ships sailing to the Islands, and altogether the best facilities for getting there. So we will start from Tilbury Docks, go down Channel, across the Bay of Biscay, through the Straits of Gibraltar, down the Mediterranean to Port Said, through the Suez Canal, down the Red Sea, over to Colombo, across the Indian Ocean, round Cape Leeuwin, across the Great Australian Bight (which is worse than the Bay of Biscay), through Bass Straits, and up the coast of New South Wales to Sydney—in one sentence that covers six weeks of fast steaming. And we shall only stay in Sydney long enough to fit ourselves out with the lightest of light clothing, and such other articles of outfit as are necessities in the Islands. They are few and they are simple.

Always and for ever, to anyone who has been in Sydney, remains one abiding impression. The city itself is a fine one— perhaps as large, or a little larger, than Liverpool—with notable buildings, many and well-kept parks, the most beautiful of Botanic Gardens, and all the twentieth-century contrivances of civilization which a great city should have, and which some in Europe that one could mention have not. But it is not Sydney that photographs itself indelibly upon one's mind. It is the Harbour—that splendid lake of gleaming blue waters, of wooded points and dazzling white beaches, of villas and gardens nestling round little bays, of great ships and little ships, of flitting yachts, of darting ferry-boats that skim like water-bugs from shore to shore, of blue, cloudless skies and brilliant sunshine, and grey men-o'-war in Farm Cove. Plenty of people have tried to describe Sydney Harbour, and none have done so adequately. There are others in the world

# Out of Sydney

just as safe, and in some respects more beautiful—some of these, that are not in the guide-books, we shall see in the Solomons and New Hebrides—but Port Jackson has a charm of its own that is peculiarly its own. Perhaps it is its blending with Sydney itself that gives it such a charm—the intermixing of bay and city, wooded point, and promontory, and suburban garden, the mingling of the romance of commerce and trade with the romance of tranquil beauty and serene peacefulness. The trains bringing wool, and mutton, and grain shunt and whistle about the quays and jetties of busy Darling Harbour ; upon Glebe Island they slaughter cattle in the abattoirs ; Balmain has its foundries ; Cockatoo Island its great docks ; the Circular Quay and Wooloomooloo Bay rattle with derricks, donkey-engines, and the feverish handling of cargo all day long ; Garden Island has its great naval works and arsenal— and yet there is never a trace or suggestion of sordidness, nothing that ever reminds one of Shadwell, or the West India Docks, or the Isle of Dogs, or the Mersey, or the Clyde. A great trade is getting itself carried on all about. The rush of business ebbs and flows in the city and along the wharves. The sea-roads lead outwards to all the world. But alone remains to one the charm of the beauty and the peace of the Harbour. You may become tired of the oft-repeated question in Sydney, " What do you think of our Harbour ?" but you will never weary of remembering it.

In the evening, as the sun goes down, up the Paramatta River, in a glory of crimson, gold, and orange, we put to sea. Our little steamer—some 1,200 tons, or thereabouts, and owned by the great Island trading firm of B. P. and Company—has a litter about the decks, and an air of being shoved off against her will. But she swings out into the fairway, and the crowd along the wharf grows indistinguishable in the fast-gathering dusk—there is little twilight in Australia—as she slowly steams down the harbour to the Heads, gathering way as she glides past the little old fort on Pinchgut, and slipping into darkness and night as she passes Bradley's Head, where the Harbour bends, and the Heads themselves begin to open out. Past the lightship on the Sow and Pigs reef, that lies just inside the entrance of Watson's Bay, and she begins to curtsy gently to the long swell that heaves in from the Tasman Sea. A few points to starboard, and we face the grey, open waters and the dimly seen horizon. Up to the left, at the top of the Harbour's northern arm, twinkle the lights of Manly Beach. Closer, under the shelter of North Head, are the lights of the Quarantine Station. High up on South Head above the Gap—where was wrecked the *Dunbar*—flashes and winks the great revolving lamp of the main light-house. An indistinct creaming of foam surges about the bases of the high sandstone cliffs. We pass through the narrow Heads, bearing gently to the swell, swing round to the Nor'-West, and head for The Black Islands—bidding farewell to cities and railway trains, telephones and tramways, newspapers and news of the older world—and set our course for those old, mysterious Islands of Dreams; out of the Twentieth Century into the days of Mendana, and far and far away beyond, into the times of Primitive Man.

The grey waters become black; the creaming foam that fizzes along the ship's side glows with phosphorescent light; the stars twinkle and burn in the clear sky overhead. A little cold head-wind sends us aft of the deckhouse for shelter and the better enjoyment of our pipes, and we stand gazing at the long, swinging electric beam of the South Head Light, as it falls astern and astern, until it is time to go below for the evening meal, and to make the acquaintance of the returning traders, an odd missionary or two, an assistant-commissioner, and the several nondescripts of our own kind whose names make up the passenger list.

In three days we shall touch at Lord Howe's Island, and in six at Norfolk Island—our good ship is not exactly an ocean greyhound.

CRUISING AMONG THE SOUTH SEA ISLANDS

# Norfolk Island

## CHAPTER III

### NORFOLK ISLAND

It is almost possible to take in Lord Howe's Island, as the French would say, at a single " blow of the eye," so tiny is it, and so steep and rugged. It has, of course, nothing to do with Melanesia, save that it lies on the road from Sydney to the Western Pacific. Scarcely three miles long by about half a mile wide, it supports, fairly comfortably, some fifty to sixty persons, who live by fishing and farming. There is about it, however, one rather interesting fact for European readers. There is indigenous, and there only, the beautiful little dwarf palm which ornaments so many tables in the older world— the *Kentia*. A firm of Sydney florists has a large garden in the island in which the palms are carefully cultivated, and from it the seeds are sent out all over the world.

Norfolk Island, on the other hand, although situated in a vast and lonely waste of waters, and some hundreds of miles from its southern limits, has a direct and important connection with Melanesia, for there are established the head-quarters of the English Diocese of Melanesia, and those of the Melanesian Mission. But apart from that—in its history and its people, its extraordinary beauty and fertility, it is one of the most interesting and fascinating little islands in the South Seas.

Nearly every schoolboy must know the story of the mutiny in H.M.S. *Bounty*. Those who don't should get to know it, for it is a most enthralling and romantic narrative of fact. One always has regrets that Captain Marryat did not handle the amazing story as it should have been handled. It has been used by other writers—and notably well in a novel called " The Mutineers "—but only Marryat could have done it justice. The tyranny and hazing that led to the desperate seizure of a King's Ship, the splendid achievement of Captain Bligh in navigating his open boat, and the few faithful who stood by him, over 3,000 miles of tempestuous sea to Timor, and the strange story of the mutineers themselves—a story that is not yet finished—are material for one of the most interesting yarns that has ever been told. How the mutineers returned to Tahiti, took wives from amongst the natives, sailed to little Pitcairn Island, burned the *Bounty*, founded a colony and a race of people as unique as any in the world, quarrelled, fought, killed one another, and finally throve and multiplied until Pitcairn was too small to hold them, and then were brought to Norfolk Island in 1857, between sixty and seventy years after the mutiny—is it not written ? But it has never been written quite so well as it should have been.

The descendants of the mutineers who are living to-day in Norfolk Island are as strange and singular to the average Englishman as a Lancashire " laad " is to a Cockney. They have a quaint language, compounded, as far as an outsider can gather, of Tahitian, sailor-slang, and English. Its grammatical structure must very much resemble that of the Boer " Taal." Their soft, gentle, caressing voices, intensely musical, remind one of their Tahitian extraction, and their natural courtesy and kindliness would seem to have come also from the far-off Eastern Pacific. It may be that they will lie to you, and they may abuse you and laugh at you when your back is turned, but they will never be rude to you. A free, open-hearted hospitality to the stranger is one of their most marked characteristics ; but if he goes and lives among them, and they discover that they do not like him, they are capable of making it so hot for him that he will be glad to leave the Island. In many ways they are eminently contradictory in character, but to anyone who takes people as he finds them, and treats them decently himself, they cannot fail to appear altogether attractive and charming.

# Norfolk Island

It is a curiously independent little community, having its own separate existence as a kind of Crown colony. The Governor of the State of New South Wales is also its Governor, and there is a resident magistrate who is nominated by him ; but they have their own miniature parliament, in the shape of an Elective Council of Elders. There are no taxes, except customs duties on a few more or less luxurious articles of commerce, such as tobacco. It is strictly a prohibition State, and no one may import or possess alcohol save by the permission of the Resident Medical Officer. In place of taxes, every able-bodied man is compelled to work for so many days in the year upon the roads which traverse the Island—relics of the old convict regime—or else find a substitute to do so. They live by farming, grazing, fishing, and whaling. Every year, and at almost exactly the same time of the year, the whales make their appearance off the Island. Some time in May or June they may be looked for with certainty, and they remain in the vicinity until October or November. The Islanders hunt them vigorously, and there is no finer day's sport to be had anywhere than a day's whaling with these wonderful boatmen. There is not so much fun, to be sure, in assisting to tow the whale back to the Island—but " that is another story."

The Melanesian Mission—with its houses for the clergy, its schools for native teachers brought down from the Islands, its model farm, its hospital, and the beautiful Patteson Memorial Chapel—occupies about 1,000 acres of the Island. Its whole extent is about 8,000 acres, and, roughly, including the *Bounty* people, as they are called, the clergy, helpers, Melanesian natives at the Mission, and the staff at the Pacific Cable Station, the population is a little over 1,000 souls. But even these figures do not impress one with an idea of the Island's wonderful fertility so much as the fact that, in the days of the convict settlement, it supported nearly 3,000 prisoners, officials, and soldiers.

# The South Seas

It is a paradise of peace and beauty to-day, but not much more than half a century ago Norfolk Island was such a hell upon earth as has, fortunately, seldom been known before. It was a depot, or rather a dumping-ground, for the scum and the dregs of the convict establishments in Australia and Tasmania. The old prisons and barracks and factories still stand, and in the gloomy and decaying ruins of the prisons one may read to-day the miseries and cruelties of the stern and pitiless regime that once held sway in the Island. In the most powerful Australian novel that has yet been written—Marcus Clark's "For the Term of His Natural Life"—you may read, with no fears as to exaggeration, one of the best accounts of this cruel chapter in the Island's history. If anything, its horrors are understated, for there were some that, for very decency, no publisher could print, but that it is a truthful picture there are still living people who can vouch. We will soon be in New Caledonia—and, if a French penal settlement "ain't all your fancy paints," it is well to remember that Noumea and Isle Nou are to what Norfolk Island *was* as a young ladies' boarding-school is to a criminal lunatic asylum.

But that sad and dreary chapter is closed, and we must take Norfolk Island as we find it to-day—a little heaven—and try to forget that it was ever a little hell. Of its beauty there could be no possible exaggeration. Lying away by itself in the midst of the Great Deep, it is just like a well-kept English park planted down in the wide Pacific. Little valleys and rolling ridges, covered with the greenest of greensward, make up the contour of the Island. Pleasant brooks trickle down the valleys to the sea. Mount Pitt rises to somewhere about 1,000 feet near the centre of the Island, and from its summit the view is something to remember and treasure. At your feet the wonderful little land flowing with milk and honey, and all about you, like the view from a ship's mast, the vast blue circle of sea, limited by the blue dome of the sky. Everywhere grows the pine peculiar to the Island (*Araucaria excelsa*), a

# Norfolk Island

splendid and a stately tree. You will find it also growing in
little pots in houses in England—a perfect model of its gigantic
brother in the South Pacific—but to see it at its best and
grandest you must see it in its own beautiful home. Oranges
grow wild all over the Island, and there are great groves of
lemon everywhere. As you ride along the roads you may
pick huge luscious guavas, and there never were such straw-
berries as the Islanders grow in their gardens. Every kind of
European fruit flourishes, and side by side with them stand
banana plantations and sweet-potato patches. As has been
said of it, " No one need work in Norfolk Island ; let him just
sit down in the sun with his mouth open, and he will be fed."
And as a pure matter of fact, no one *does* work there very
much.

## CHAPTER IV

### THE PRISON ISLAND

FROM Norfolk Island our course lies almost due north to
Noumea, the capital of New Caledonia, across some 300 miles
of open water. As we approach the south-eastern end of the
Island, we first of all become aware of the long line of breaking
surf that marks the coral reef which stretches almost all round
New Caledonia. Coasting along it, up the eastern side, we
soon sight a tall white lighthouse, standing, apparently, in the
sea behind the line of surf. It is uncanny in its solitude.
When we come abreast of it our course is altered slightly to the
westward, and we glide through the passage in the reef which
it is set to mark, and continue, in calm waters, up to the
entrance to Noumea Harbour, the blue coast-line gradually
taking definite form of cliff and beach, hill and valley, with
a backing of high mountain ranges in the distance. The

13

# The South Seas

harbour is a very fine one, almost completely land-locked, and safe in any weather. On our way up to the quayside at the town itself, we pass Isle Nou—that dreadful, orderly inferno where are confined in a grim prison the most desperate and abandoned of the desperate exiles who form the main part of the population of New Caledonia.

About the middle of the last century New Caledonia was acquired by the French, and it was not long before the transportation of criminals from France began. Since then it has been continuously a penal settlement, and hardly anything else, although during recent years transportation has been discontinued, mainly owing to the representations of the Australian Government. But even the suspension of transportation has little altered the general character of the place, since a large proportion of the criminals sent from France is, after the completion of the prison term, compelled under the class of sentence received to remain in New Caledonia or its dependencies. These *libérés*, or, as we should say, ticket-of-leave men, have often developed into good and useful colonists, and in some cases have acquired considerable wealth; but more often they remain what they seem to have been destined to be from the beginning—the dregs of society.

Almost from a first glance at the place Noumea impresses the visitor with an unmistakable notion of what it is. First, there are the walled buildings, barracks and penitentiaries, upon Isle Nou. At the wharf one perceives parties of prisoners under armed guards doing various kinds of government or municipal work. In the evenings great barges, packed to overflowing with gaunt men, are towed across the harbour to Isle Nou from various public works on the mainland where they have slaved all day. In the roads about the town one passes large bodies of them marching to or from work in "fours"—unhappy, gaunt men, with pallid, starved-looking countenances that are savage, stolid, sorrowful, cunning, or desperate, but always unhappy. To English eyes there is

14

# The Prison Island

something a little ludicrous in the aspect of one of these gangs at work—something that takes away for the moment from the tragedy and misery of it ; for the guards, burly and rather genial-looking prison warders, dressed in white duck, and having a huge revolver strapped to girths that very frequently show the curves of good living, stroll about supervising the work beneath the shelter of enormous cotton " ginghams." One speculates as to what would become of the umbrellas in the event of a rush of prisoners, when they would have to be thrown aside for the better manipulation of the big revolvers.  An English resident of Noumea, however, told the writer that he once witnessed an unfortunate prisoner make an attempt to dash into some adjacent scrub from a road-making party when he thought the vigilance of the guards was relaxed.  One of the latter, a very stout man, sweltering in the heat of a glaring day beneath an enormous sunshade, coolly shifted its handle from his right hand to his left, drew his revolver, and deftly " potted " the running man at a distance of twenty or thirty yards without moving from the rock upon which he was sitting.

Although everywhere the prison aspect of Noumea forces itself upon one, the town itself is picturesque, and even cheerful.  Frequent cafés line the sidewalks of streets, that are usually named after some French victory or other—as Rue Austerlitz, Rue Inkerman, or Rue Sebastopol.  It is on record, in this connection, that some essentially boorish English visitor was once challenged to a duel for remarking that he was unable to find either the Rue Waterloo or the Rue Sedan.  In the middle of the town is a fine open space—Cocoanut Square—surrounded by brilliant flame-trees, and having in the midst a band-stand and a group of statuary.  With a kind of grim humour, or else a most deplorable lack of it, the statuary is symbolical of Liberty, and is so labelled.  In the evenings a fine band, whose members are all convicts, occasionally occupies the band-stand, and discourses sweet music to those

15

who sit at the little tables outside the surrounding cafés. The market-place, in another part of the town, is a busy and animated scene in the early mornings, where housewives, housekeepers, and cooks bargain vigorously for meat, vegetables, fruit, fish, eggs, and various and sundry articles of clothing and light merchandise. The fish are brought alive in wheeled open tanks filled with salt water, and you may select part of your *déjeuner* whilst it is swimming about alive. There is a fine cathedral on an eminence at the back of the town, and outside it stands—perhaps also a little incongruously—a statue of Joan of Arc in armour. Liberté and Jeanne d'Arc, as the sole public statuary of Noumea, seem just a little like " rubbing it in " to the greater part of the population of the town.

New Caledonia itself is one of the finest and best islands in the South Pacific. It is rich in minerals, and well suited for both grazing and agriculture. The climate is temperate, and the rainfall sufficiently abundant. On the whole, one receives the impression that it is greatly wasted in its present situation. Politically, it is somewhat of an eyesore to Australia, from the fact of its existence as a naval base and arsenal so close to the shores of the Commonwealth. A large garrison, out of all proportion in numbers to the necessities of guarding and keeping order amongst the convict population, is maintained by France, and the harbour is strongly and extensively fortified. It is a curious fact that a large number of the free French residents would prefer to see the Island handed over to England. Some reason for this may perhaps be found in the existence of the heavy Australian tariff, which effectually closes their most natural market against merchants and producers. The feeling manifested itself in 1907 in a petition presented to the French Home Government, and signed by many influential French residents, praying that some kind of " deal " might be made with England, whereby New Caledonia would become a British possession.

SCENERY IN EROMANGA, NEW HEBRIDES

# The New Hebrides : Port Vila

The natives of New Caledonia and the Loyalty Islands to the east of it—also in the possession of France—are of the true Melanesian type, whom we shall be enabled to observe more closely and fully in the New Hebrides and Solomon groups. In the 'Seventies they rebelled against French rule, and a bloody and disastrous rising occurred, which was finally so effectively put down by the French troops that the native population has ceased to count for very much since, and may be regarded as entirely subjugated and abject. Most of the recruited native "labour" is obtained from the Loyalty Islands, whose inhabitants would seem to have a better liking and a greater aptitude for work than the New Caledonians.

## CHAPTER V

### THE NEW HEBRIDES : PORT VILA

A SPLENDID wide bay of horseshoe shape ; long, wooded arms that run by either side towards the open sea ; clear, calm blue waters stretching between ; here and there the gleaming roofs of planter's bungalow or mission-station ; at the head, fringing along a white beach, backed by dense primeval forest, and nestling among palms and tree-ferns, and luxuriant vines and flowers, the little township which the English call Vila and the French Franceville ; and over all a blue sky and hot sunlight— Port Vila, the principal centre of the New Hebrides, and so far as trade goes, also the principal centre of the whole of Melanesia.

If you turn back to the map you will see, about half-way between the large islands of Erromango to the northward, and Malekula, or Mallicollo, to the north, a little island called Vate, or Sandwich. (You will not forget, if you please, the author's humble warning in the first chapter as to the conning of maps and charts of the South Sea Islands.) Sandwich, as it is generally spoken of, is not nearly such a little duck-roost as it appears to be. It has several very good and safe harbours, rivers, and high mountain ranges in the interior. On the eastern, or south-eastern, side of it, at the head of its beautiful bay, lies Vila—or, as we should speak of it if this book were written in French for French readers, Franceville. But since we write in English for English readers, we will allude to it always by the name it is most frequently referred to under by Englishmen in Melanesia.

Vila is a place of considerable importance—of much greater importance than you would suppose, as you enter the harbour and see it for the first time. Not only is it the seat of Government in the New Hebrides—that quaint and ambiguous form known as the Dual Control—it is also a meeting-place for several important South Sea Island trade routes. As well as those which radiate through Melanesia, a good many of the Polynesian and Micronesian roads converge upon it. Colombo in Ceylon (or is it Port Said ?) has been spoken of as the Clapham Junction of the Far East. Although Vila is scarcely a Clapham Junction, it might not inaptly be called the Willesden Junction of the South Seas. It is "Change here for the Banks, Torres, Santa Cruz, and Solomon groups—all change for Fiji, Rotumah, Ellice, Gilbert, and Marshall Islands—junction for Noumea and Loyalties." A gentleman in uniform, up a cocoa-nut tree, making such an announcement through a speaking-trumpet to an in-coming ship would not be nearly so absurd as he would seem. But more important than all, it is the head-quarters of Messrs. Burns, Philp, and Company. Although in these days gratuitous advertisement is unusual and undesirable, one cannot possibly deal with Melanesia without referring to the great trading firm which has done so much towards the development and civilizing of the Islands in their latter-day history. If one were not

# The New Hebrides : Port Vila

to do so one might just as consistently ignore missionaries, traders, men-o'-war, and resident commissioners.

To look at this little leaf-bowered village—a handful of houses on the edge of a tropical jungle—you would hardly suppose that politics of high importance, international politics, could centre in it. But so it is. There are questions relating to Vila which disturb and perplex both Whitehall, the Quai D'Orsay, and the Commonwealth Parliament in Melbourne. They are questions which have perplexed responsible people in or about those three places for no little while, and are likely to continue in the propagation of perplexity ; but which some day will have to be settled definitely, and for good or evil to the Islands. There is not space here to enter into their discussion with any completeness, if at all, nor does the scope of this book allow of their discussion, but they are very vital in Vila.

To understand anything as to the condition of the New Hebrides, however, it is necessary to consider the Dual Control. The group is under the joint "protection" of France and England, and is locally ruled by two resident commissioners, French and English, who exercise, or are supposed to exercise, equal powers. That such a system possesses grave short-comings—however good it may be in theory—must be immediately obvious to all who have ever had to do with, or seen anything of, the control of native races, and particularly of savage native races. However capable, painstaking, and honourable the resident authorities may be, their courses *must* sometimes run counter to one another, there *must* be friction. The interests of their respective countrymen must frequently clash, and their ideas as to methods of dealing with their common charge—their notion as to the best way of carrying " the White Man's Burden "—cannot but be often at variance. And such a condition of things is no less a hindrance to the prosperity of the Dual Protectorate than it is inimical to the welfare of the natives and the maintenance of order. We

19                         3—2

cannot go deeply into the question here, but it may be permissible to institute a comparison, at least so far as regards the maintenance of order, between the New Hebrides and the British Solomon Islands. In the latter, which are ruled in undivided authority by a single Resident Commissioner, with two or three assistants, intertribal fighting and bloodshed are infinitely rarer than in the former. Land on a beach in the New Hebrides, and you will see every second or third native carrying firearms. In the Solomons an effective rifle is the exception. Fighting amongst the natives themselves, and the sport of missionary murder, are rarer in what ought to be the much more savage Solomons than in these islands. And one cannot but believe that the worse condition of the New Hebrides is directly traceable to the farcical system of a double government. A " nigger " can understand one " boss," but two are one too many for him. And this applies to all " niggers."

If you stand on the rising ground behind B. P.'s store at Vila, or in the garden of the quarters occupied by B. P.'s officials, and look down the harbour towards the sea at sunset, you will gaze upon such a glory of colour and beauty as you will never forget. Below the store, and out beyond the little landing-stage, stretch the calm waters of the bay, gleaming with all the tints and iridescent lights of mother-o'-pearl or opal. Where the reefs lie shoal the hues of the coral show through the waters. Clear, deep green, mirrored reflections of jungle and palm darken the surface along either arm of the horseshoe. Two or three trim white schooners lie at anchor close in shore. Up to the left, perhaps, one of His Britannic Majesty's grey cruisers rides at her moorings. Not far from her is a white French gunboat. Far to seaward the setting sun gilds the dancing waters. It is a wonderfully beautiful scene—too beautiful for adequate description.

It happened one evening that the author dined in Vila. It happened, also, that of half a dozen people at the table he alone was clean shaved. The host carved a joint, and two dusky, mop-headed New Hebridean maidens waited upon the guests. Mentioning the author's name, the host directed one of these ladies to convey a helping to him. The lady was puzzled, and did not seem to know whom the plate might be intended for. Immediately the host enlightened her : " You give it that feller no grass longa face."

There you have a little bit of Melanesian pigeon-English. You will hear more of it before you get back to Sydney.

## CHAPTER VI

### THE COMING OF THE WHITE MAN

AND now the author is about to state a somewhat astonishing fact, which you may or may not believe, but which is, nevertheless, a serious statement of fact alone.

The finding of the New Hebrides took the best part of three centuries to complete, and the navigators of three great nations to complete it. It is curious to remember that during these three centuries Spain, France, and England—the nations to whose hardy and skilful sailors the credit of discovering the group belongs—were for the most part at deadly enmity with one another. From near the times of the Armada to the Napoleonic Wars brave and daring mariners of the three peoples groped and searched those far-off seas, returned home to make quaint reports and quainter maps, or disappeared in the mysterious Southern Ocean, often without leaving the slightest trace or record of their inscrutable fate.

To the Spaniards of our Elizabethan age is due our first knowledge of Melanesia, and a few years later that of part of the New Hebrides. They were the first white men to visit the Solomon Islands. They found Santa Cruz (how many Santa

# The South Seas

Cruzes have the Spaniards found ?), the Banks Islands, and a little bit of the New Hebrides. Later, the French explored and increased the general knowledge of the Spaniards' discoveries. Then came the English, who sounded, and surveyed, and charted, and helped themselves to large portions of the new lands. But the honours of the earliest and most interesting discoveries remain with Spain.

Later on in this book, when we are in the Solomons, we will look back to Mendana's wonderful voyage from Peru, and his still more wonderful explorations in and about the islands which he found for Spain, and which Spain was never able to find again. But in this chapter we are only concerned with the New Hebrides. Mendana made two voyages—the first in 1567, and the second, which was undertaken with a view to colonizing his discoveries, in 1595. His project was a failure whose tragedy was accentuated by his own death. But as the outcome of his failure Fernandez de Quiros found the New Hebrides.

Quiros had sailed with Mendana, and shared with him the disappointments and miseries which attended the luckless and short-lived colony at Graciosa Bay in Santa Cruz. He was, however, more fortunate than his leader, and returned alive to Peru. The glamour of the Islands—that strange hankering after them which still besets those who have once been in their midst—must have possessed him strongly, for during ten years he never ceased in his efforts to induce, first the Viceroy of Peru, and then the Court itself, to make good the work of Mendana, and turn the " Isles of Salomon " to the glory and the uses of Spain. After ten long years of pertinacious endeavour and heart-breaking disappointment (much the same thing as Columbus had to endure), he was furnished with two ships, and sailed from Callao in 1605, with Luis Vaez de Torres as second in command, to make new search for the Solomons. He steered in the direction of Santa Cruz, but passed it to the northward, and came to some small islands, which, 200 years afterwards, were named the Duff group. From them, after a short rest, he turned southward, and quite unwittingly missed the island of San Cristoval, and so, also, his chance of rediscovering the Solomons. Equally unfortunate was he with regard to Santa Cruz, which he passed without seeing. But at length he was rewarded, in his imagination, by a great discovery. For years the legend of a vast southern continent had fired the hopes of the old navigators, and when Quiros dropped anchor in a bay in the coast of a large island, he was flushed with pride in the belief that his years of endeavour had at length been crowned with a success more dazzling than had attended the efforts of any of his predecessors. So he named it Tierra Austral del Espiritu Santo (the Southern Land of the Holy Ghost). But here again, in the moment of his supposed triumph, his luck deserted him. His crew mutinied, forced him to put to sea in the night without permitting him to communicate with Torres in the other ship, and finally to return to Mexico. It was left to Torres to find out that Santo (as it is now called) was an island. Then he sailed westward, passed between the real Southern Continent and New Guinea, by the straits that bear his name, and at length arrived at Manilla in the Philippine Islands.

Poor, brave, strenuous Fernandez de Quiros! He never lost his dream of a new Spain in southern seas. Year after year he made unwearied effort to induce the Court to send him forth again in quest of the Isles of Salomon and the Australia del Espiritu Santo—fruitlessly for long, but never without hope that his dream might be realized. Fifty petitions he presented to the King, and in one of them, after glowingly describing the riches, beauty, and fertility (who would not so describe them ?) of his beloved islands, he thus apostrophizes him : " Acquire, sire, since you can, acquire heaven, eternal fame, and that new world with all its promises." At length, when an old man, his appeals were granted, and in 1614, carrying the King's Commission, he sailed from Spain on his way to Callao, to fit out another expedition. But he died at Panama, and with him died all Spanish enterprise in the Western Pacific. A brave life ended at the pestilential isthmus. It was to such men as Quiros that Spain owed the one-time greatness of her vast colonial Empire. Where is it now—" Where are the snows of Yesterday ?"

The Spaniards came, and looked, and went away, and never came again—but what a mighty If there is about it! If the dream of Quiros had been realized, Australia might to-day have been a second Brazil or Peru—possibly it might still have been a Spanish province, but it is more likely that it would have been an independent and revolutionary republic. The mutiny at Santo made no little difference to the present-day extent of the British Empire.

In the slow course of the centuries the New Hebrides have gradually become known. Captain Cook discovered their principal islands. La Pérouse met a fate which was not known until years afterwards on a reef at Vanikoro, and disappeared utterly from the ken of mankind. The whalers came. Then the " blackbirders," and the traders. Finally, the settlers—but the years to come contain the " Finally."

Cook it was who named the group " New Hebrides." Now, Cook was a very great man, and a very great sailor, and the writer yields to nobody in admiration for him ; but he certainly was a duffer at bestowing names upon his discoveries. The New Hebrides, in their tropical gorgeousness, are about as like the bleak Old Hebrides as the island in the Serpentine is like Teneriffe. Such a designation is, however, quite in keeping with his clumsy name for the east coast of Australia— New South Wales—and his commonplace christening of the beautiful harbour of Sydney as " Port Jackson."

A YAM SHED AND NATIVES
ESPIRITU SANTO, NEW HEBRIDES

# The New Hebrideans

## CHAPTER VII

### THE NEW HEBRIDEANS

THE native of the New Hebrides differs considerably from the aboriginal inhabitant of neighbouring groups of islands. He is darker than the Fijian, not so well built or graceful, less intelligent, and less prepossessing—but, on the other hand, physically, at any rate, he excels the Solomon Islander. There is something in his appearance that reminds one of the Australian native, but if there is really a resemblance it is merely a superficial one. To liken him in other respects to that hopeless and degraded type of humanity would be to libel him in a particularly bad fashion. It is possible that he is naturally more savage than his neighbour in the Solomons—despite the latter's penchant for head-hunting, and his hardly eradicated attribute of cannibalism—but in a certain sense he is more civilized. That is to say, he has come more into touch with civilization. Whether such contact with the outer world has been of much benefit to him is another matter.

But in spite of whatever differences may distinguish the New Hebridean from the native of Santa Cruz or the Solomons, we can only consider him here as being essentially a Melanesian —just as we broadly class those very different types, the Yorkshireman and the Cornishman, as English. Every island possesses its own characteristics. Variations in language and custom are abundant. Dialects differ all through the groups. Social usages, habits, domestic arts, weapons, and traditions are localized everywhere. But a relationship of race, language, and custom extends through, and unites ethnologically, the whole of Melanesia. A native of the group is a Melanesian before he is a New Hebridean.

# The South Seas

All through the South Seas, and even including the great continent of Australia itself, a fog of mystery enshrouds the beginnings of the races that people them. Before the fifteenth century we know them not at all. Greece was great, Rome rose to the zenith of her power and glory and declined, Christianity changed the world, nations and empires waxed and waned, the history we read to-day was made—and these far-off seas slept through the rain and sunshine of the ages, with their story unwritten and their chronicles unrecorded. We know nothing to-day of what was happening in the South Pacific about the time, say, when Cæsar landed on the beach near Deal. We can pretty correctly surmise that the Melanesian dug his yams and cultivated his banana patches, went fishing off his reefs and beaches, raided his neighbours' villages, and was raided by his neighbours, went head-hunting and was an occasional cannibal, as he was 350 years ago when the Spaniards found him—but we can go no farther than that. Where he came from, and when, we do not know, and we never shall. Consider that in the Solomons such a notable and impressive thing as the coming of the first white man has not left even the shadow of a memory in the native mind, and you will realize how short tradition must be with the native, how very much existence is a matter of the present alone to him. He practises ancestor worship, it is true, but it is very little, if anything at all, that he knows concerning his great-grandfather. He has his legends and his fairy tales, but no element of chronology enters into them. All that he knows of the Past is that it is a vague, indefinite period that preceded his own. He has no particular interest in it, and not a shred of curiosity concerning it. His origin is unknown to him, and the fact that it is unknown worries him not at all. Like Topsy, he is of opinion that he " jest growed."

There are certain things that may be deduced from their present condition that go a little way—a very little way— towards the tracing of the genesis of the Melanesians. The

# The New Hebrideans

variety of the languages they use, and differences in habits and arts, prove that they did not all come together into the islands that they now inhabit. The same root language is embodied in all their dialects; there is a broad likeness in their religious beliefs and observances, and their habits of life and social usages, that connect them generally; but in detail there are great and remarkable differences. It may be possible some day, when they are better known, and their ways have been studied for a longer time, that their origin may be dimly traced, and some light thrown upon their connection with the outer world. But the one certain fact remains to-day that neither black man nor white man knows anything about the beginnings of the Melanesian as a race, nor of the New Hebrideans as a division of the race.

For his own beginnings, however, and the beginnings of his world, the Melanesian has many and picturesque ways of accounting. His legendary lore is wide and varied. The making of man, the finding of fish, bird stories and beast stories, the adventures of disembodied spirits, the doings of ghosts—the whole romantic aspect of the supernatural is contained in his fairy tales. There are wonderful stories concerning a rather benevolent being of the spiritual world called Qatu or Qat, of whom we shall go into particulars later on. In the meantime here is the story of how Tagaro the Little made the Sea. The story is told in the island of Aurora, which you will find in the map due east of Santo in the New Hebrides. The translation—a very literal one—is given by the Rev. Dr. Codrington, in his fascinating book "The Melanesians":

"They say that he made the sea, and that in old times the sea was quite small, like a common pool upon the beach, and that this pool was at the back of his house, and that there were fish in the pool, and that he had built a stone wall round it. And Tagaro was gone out to look at the various things he had made, and his wife was in the village, and his two children were at home, whom he had forbidden to go to the back of the house. So when he was gone the thought entered into the mind of those two, Why has our father forbidden us to go there? And they were shooting at lizards and rats; and after a while one said to the other, Let us go and see what that is he has bid us keep away from. So they went and saw the pool of salt-water with many fish crowding together in it. And one of the boys stood on the stones Tagaro had built up, and he sees the fish, and he shoots at one and hits it; and as he runs to catch hold of it he threw down a stone, and then the water ran out. And Tagaro heard the roaring of the water, and ran to stop it; and the old woman laid herself down in the way of it, but nothing could be done; those two boys who had thrown down the stone took clubs, little knives, and prepared a passage for the sea, one on one side and the other on the other side of the place, and the sea followed as it flowed. And they think that the old woman turned into a stone, and lies now in the part of Maewo (Aurora) near Raga."

This Tagaro was a redoubtable little sprite, and, like most of the Melanesian's favourite mythical personages, rather a good soul than otherwise. He did a whole lot of useful things, after the fashion of the making of the sea, and was a very clever fellow in every respect. Tales of his exploits are common throughout Melanesia, but he seems to be at the height of his popularity with the New Hebrideans.

## CHAPTER VIII

### THE NEW HEBRIDEANS (*continued*)

BUT—perhaps because the grapes are sour—we will leave the beginnings of the Melanesians alone, and consider the present condition of the native people of the New Hebrides.

Roughly speaking, the natives of the group may be said to be in a transition stage—just the commencement of it. The influence of the white man, both for good and evil, is beginning to make its results noticeable. Especially has this been the case within the last few years, during which the white population has almost doubled itself. And it is most curious to note how here—perhaps more than in any other country peopled by savages—the white man's influence has been divided up into classes which, if not actually at variance with one another, are as dissimilar as it is possible for them to be. In methods of colonization we have both English and French. In methods of Christianizing, we have those of the followers of John Wesley and of the Church of Rome. Here, in the very essentials of the process of civilization, we find influences brought to bear upon the native that are utterly unlike, if not to a certain degree hostile to, one another. It would be strange if some small amount of chaos did not manifest itself in these earlier stages.

It is not, of course, to be supposed that French or English, Roman Catholics or Wesleyans, are bitterly opposed to one another, or that there is to any extent a persistent effort on the part of nation or sect to undermine or destroy the influence and the efforts of " the other party." As a matter of fact there is generally an excellent spirit of fellowship between English and French planters and traders, while, if the bitternesses that exist the world over between the teachers of one faith and another exist in the New Hebrides, it is cheering to be able to record that, as between man and man, the missionaries of the older and newer forms of Christianity " play the game." But the effect upon the native of these totally unlike influences must be peculiar. To put it as mildly as possible, he must be a little puzzled and uncertain. Between English and French he gets firearms and " square-face " (gin), and between Catholic and ultra-Protestant he acquires a queer blend of Christianity.

There is yet another influence that counts for a good deal—the effect of the much abused, and not very defensible, labour traffic between the Islands and the Queensland sugar plantations. Kanaka labour has lately been abolished in the Commonwealth of Australia, and " blackbirding " is almost a thing of the past, but those natives who have had the experience of a term on the plantations have often returned to their homes to practise some of the white man's virtues, even if they have acquired some of his vices. For one thing, they have, in many cases, learned the advantages to be derived from an intelligent cultivation of the soil.

As an effect of these influences, diverse as they are, many of the ancient and barbarous customs of the natives are dying out. It is a pity that some of their more harmless usages should disappear, as they must inevitably do in the coming years, but a matter for congratulation that such horrible and ghastly practices as the burying alive of their old people are beginning to fall into abeyance. The last-named horror still has being in some islands, but it can only be the matter of a generation or so before it is numbered with the things forgotten. That it lingers still is, curiously enough, mainly due to the predilections of the old people themselves. The great ambition and delight of a New Hebridean native is to possess a firearm of some kind. Unscrupulous traders—without prejudice, one believes them to have been more

# The New Hebrideans

often French than English—have not hesitated to make handsome profits in trade by bartering arms and ammunition for various articles of island produce. As a result, in many of the islands the native population is most fearfully and wonderfully equipped with a strange and diverse assortment of more or less ancient firearms, which, as a rule, are generally more dangerous to marksman than target. Landing upon beaches in certain of the islands, even when the natives are on entirely friendly terms with white men, is quite a thrilling experience. Every third man who crowds down to meet your boat carries an ancient Snider—not infrequently a condemned Tower musket—in the crook of his arm, and as his pride in his weapon often induces him to carry it loaded and at full cock, it can be well understood that the most welcome visitor stands a very fair chance of being accidentally shot. It is not infrequently the case, also, that this same pride is the sole cause of savage and bloody little wars between villages and districts, in which scores of natives are wiped out. A village will find itself in the proud possession of an accumulated store of ammunition, and simply for the fun of using it up—merely in an entirely " sporting " spirit—will suddenly attack a village in some other part of the island. As a rule, the attacking village selects another which is known to be weak in the munitions of war, and a fairly horrible amount of indiscriminate bloodshed is the result. It is seldom the case that the New Hebridean is a good marksman—he could hardly be such with the ancient and decrepit weapon he usually is provided with—but he generally catches his victim at close quarters when the latter is not expecting him. It is a jest amongst white men in the group that a native war is only really a dangerous affair when the New Hebridean is fighting with his own original arms. But however true that may be, the fact remains that an immense amount of bloodshed amongst the natives themselves is the outcome of his having been provided with firearms, and it would be an excellent thing for the New Hebrides if the mere possession of a gun by a native were a highly penal offence, and the supplying of it to him by a trader a crime that would entail the severest punishment and deportation from the Islands. There are, to be sure, regulations to prevent the sale of firearms, but the unfortunate Dual Control provides many loopholes by which they may be evaded.

In their domestic arts the New Hebrideans display no small amount of skill and cunning. Their houses are generally well built and well equipped, though, as in all Melanesia, they are the usual grass and thatch structures. In canoe-building they are particularly adept, but their craft do not display the same neatness and " finish " as are to be found in those of the Solomon Islanders. They are " dug-outs " with outriggers —that is to say, they are hewn from a single solid log of wood, and provided with a heavy float secured at some little distance from the side of the canoe to the ends of poles which stretch from the gunwale to the outrigger. In handling their canoes they are very skilful indeed, and it is a wonderful sight when they paddle them through the surf at the entrance to a lagoon or in landing upon an exposed beach.

We have not space here to go very fully into the customs and habits of the New Hebridean, but in some later chapters we will be able to consider some of the more interesting social usages of the Melanesian generally. We must pass very briefly by local characteristics, and can only deal with those general ones which apply to the Melanesian as a whole.

A "DUG-OUT" WITH OUTRIGGERS

## CHAPTER IX

### THE SOLOMONS : GAVUTU

AFTER leaving Vila and the New Hebrides, the first land of the Solomons we make is the large island of San Cristoval. As we glide over the bluest of sunlit seas up its south-western coast, the massive grandeur of the towering mountain ranges in the interior, the wild primeval aspect of the dense forests that stretch downwards everywhere to the seashore, and the apparent emptiness and solitude that brood over its rugged outline, are infinitely striking. As it looks to us to-day, so must it have looked to Mendana and his Spanish sailors three and a half centuries ago. Cape and promontory open out as we sail by ; bay and harbour unfold their gorgeous panorama of tropical scenery, curving beaches and jutting reefs, headlands and little islands, pass in review before us, and over all there seems to rest the silence and mystery of many ages, the vague, unknowable secrets of the unrecorded centuries. Seldom do we see the little grass-built villages amongst the palms above the beach ; only rarely does a curl of smoke, showing like a blue spiral against the deep shadows of the mountain-side, indicate that human beings people these dark, still forests ; it is only an odd fisherman in his canoe whom we perceive now and again paddling gently over the still waters of some wide bay. Beautiful and grand as a view of it from the sea is, there is something stern and forbidding in the very aspect of San Cristoval, some tacit warning to the voyager that here is an inhospitable land, a land of danger and disaster, and the chance of sudden death.

And so, indeed, it is. San Cristoval is one of the most savage and uncivilized islands in the whole of the South Seas.

# The South Seas

A few years ago, when the author saw it, it was the only large island in the Solomon group upon which a missionary, of one denomination or another, had not established himself, nor were there any resident traders living upon it. What trade came from it was collected by the traders, in coasting cruises along its inhospitable shores, directly from the natives. It had a reputation for cannibalism and head-hunting, and the bush-native, or dweller in the interior, was said to be the wildest and most intractable human being in existence. Perhaps, having heard so much of evil concerning it, one found something sinister in its aspect from mere prejudice and fancy; but somehow it really does seem grimly forbidding, even on the finest, and brightest, and calmest of tropic mornings.

Guadalcanar, with its mighty Lion Mountain towering up almost to a height of 10,000 feet, and Malaita, dimly blue in the distance upon the starboard bow, seem almost cheerful and civilized after sombre San Cristoval. As a matter of fact, the "man-belong-bush" in both these islands is probably as disagreeable a customer as his contemporary in San Cristoval, but the "salt-water," or coast natives, have come more into touch with white men than have those of the latter island, and the nearer aspect of the islands themselves, for some reason which it would not be easy to explain, is less forbidding. At Aola, on the north-east coast of Guadalcanar, there is a delightfully situated little trading station that is very typical of the Solomon Islands. It is occupied by a certain genial Captain William P——, who is familiarly known amongst the natives as Billo. Aola (pronounced "owler") takes its name from the Aola River and an adjacent native village on the mainland, but Billo's house and store are built upon a tiny coral island that lies out about a quarter of a mile from the shore. With his schooner at anchor before it, his white dwelling-house and store gleaming through the stems of the tall coco-nut palms, his copra and ivory-nut sheds nestling beneath a huge spreading tree at the landing-place, a beach of dazzling white coral sand girdling the islet, the blue sea shining in the sunlight across the low flat level of it, Billo's little kingdom of about eight acres is such a charming fairy-land as to make one fervently envy him its possession. And when you go ashore to Billo's hospitable veranda, and Billo sings out to one of his " boys," " You go catch 'em ten fellow young fellow coco-nut," and you drink the thirst-quenching milk of a green nut, you feel still more envious of Billo and his kingdom.

But we must navigate carefully across the narrow inland sea that lies between Guadalcanar and Malaita to the Island of Florida, wherein is situated the principal port of the Solomons—Gavutu—and where the seat of government of the British Solomon Islands Protectorate is established. It is not a long way, as the crow flies, but we have to dodge the reefs that are sown so thickly hereabouts, and our course is more like the letter Z than a straight line.

Florida, as you will see by looking at the map, is quite a small island compared with the two large ones between which it lies. It is, however, the most important island at present in the whole group. Not only are the head-quarters of the Resident Commissioner in it, but also those of the Melanesian Mission, and, in addition, it is the principal trade centre, besides being a coaling station for the Navy. Formerly it was one of the most savage and bloodthirsty islands in the group, but now the natives have all been converted to Christianity. and it is perfectly safe to go about it anywhere unarmed. It was in Florida that the Spanish discoverers of the Solomons had their fiercest fighting with the natives.

The harbour of Gavutu, which is really the name of the small island in it upon which the trading station stands, is, even for a Solomon Island harbour, where all are so, very beautiful. It is quite landlocked, and safe in any weather. The anchorage is naturally just opposite the trading station,

# The South Seas

and numerous schooners and cutters lie ready to discharge their cargoes of copra, ivory nuts, pearl-shell, and other island produce into the bi-monthly steamer. The trading station—a very large one—stands back from the wharf and store sheds in the midst of a large coco-nut plantation. It is a big, two-storied, white wooden house, with a wide balcony running all round it. The owner of the station—who, by the way, is a Norwegian sea-captain hailing from the North Cape —provides quarters for the captain and mates of the various small craft which he owns, and at this time its accommodation is pretty fully taken up. Captain —— is a very fine specimen of the best kind of South Sea trader. He is altogether a striking and distinguished personality. Tall, dark, thin, with muscles of iron, he looks the strong and intellectual man he is —a great business man, a brave and skilful adventurer (in the better sense of the word), and a gentleman in the very fullest sense. He controls what is really a very large and affluent business, and his reputation throughout the islands is, with black man and white man, Government official and missionary, of the very highest. If all the traders in the South Seas were of the kind Captain —— is, the prosperity of the islands would be assured. One could hardly say too much in praise of such a man.

Away on another island in the harbour—Tulagi—are the head-quarters of the Resident Commissioner. If one did not fear to be taken seriously as rather a fulsome person, one might say equal things as to that gentleman ; but although he is a sort of absolute monarch over some 1,100 miles of islands, with nearly a quarter of a million subjects, he " doesn't advertise," and one would fear his wrath were one to under-take to do so on his behalf, and, moreover, the good results of his labours in the Protectorate speak for themselves. Perhaps better than any living man he knows Melanesia. He has spent nearly a quarter of a century in the islands, and knows and understands the natives as well as any white man

36

may understand them, and better than most. But one cannot refer to him without advising any whom our brief account of Melanesia may possibly interest in the Black Islands to read the book in which he describes some of his earlier experiences in the group.* In a future chapter we shall see more of the work of government in the British Solomon Islands.

## CHAPTER X

### THE VOYAGE OF MENDANA

THE romance of the discovery of the Solomons is so enthralling as to be worthy of the fullest possible consideration we have space for here. It is a record of brave, old-world adventure, of intrepid seamanship, of dauntless surmounting of difficulties and the daring of dangers that must have seemed almost insurmountable and overwhelming. In the history of nations it is interesting beyond measure, since it marks the limits of Spain's great era of colonial expansion, the high-water mark of her wonderful period of conquest in the New World. She had made the New World her own. The Newer World was to repulse her. The long-dreamed-of Southern Islands she was to find—and lose. And when they were found again, the Star of Spain was in its decline, and her glories and her conquests beginning to drop from her one by one.

In 1566, nearly three and a half centuries ago, the Governor of Peru, Lope Garcia de Castro, gave orders for the outfit of two ships for the discovery of a continent and various islands which it was believed existed to the westward of South America, and appointed as General in command of the expedi-

* "A Naturalist Among the Head-Hunters," by C. M. Woodford, C.M.G.

tion his nephew, Alvaro de Mendana. The office of Commander of the troops (*maestre de campo*) was given to Pedro de Ortega Valencia, and the Royal Ensign was Don Fernando Enriquez. The Chief Pilot—with whom, as chronicler of the expedition and its navigator, we have most to do—was Hernando Gallego. A hundred persons altogether—including four Franciscan friars and some servants—embarked in the two ships, and set sail from Callao on Wednesday, November 19, 1566.

It must have been a great day in Callao—a day of devout masses and intercessions, of gaudy religious processions, and altogether of such pomp and ceremony as befitted the setting forth of an expedition, not merely sanctioned, but actively inaugurated and encouraged by His Catholic Majesty Don Philip II. Imagine the scene as the voyage commenced from the port of the City of Kings—the crowds of Spanish conquerors upon the shore, confident in their successes ; the dusky Peruvian Indians, wondering what fresh devilment on the part of their harsh masters such a departure might portend ; monks, and clerics, and bright-eyed Spanish ladies—all come to wish farewell to the bold spirits who were sailing forth into the Unknown to discover the wonderful fabulous islands whence Solomon had enriched the Temple at Jerusalem. And the two high-pooped, old-time ships, with their great stern-lanterns, their gilding and quaint paint-work, and their white spread of canvas, standing out towards the sunset and the far horizon, beyond which lay what no man knew of, save by guess and surmise. Great unknown countries with stately cities and palaces, perhaps—new nations, strange beasts and birds. Whatever might lie in the Beyond, it did not matter—were not these the ships of Spain ? What was it if that impudent pirate Drake was burning, and harrying, and singeing the King's beard across the continent ? He was nothing. Spain was about to stretch forth her hands to seize new lands and new riches. The Lions of Castile sought fresh fields. And so the

# The Voyage of Mendana

two ships passed out of sight, and the darkness of the mysterious seas swallowed them.

Steering in a southerly and westerly direction, they reached the latitude of $15\frac{1}{2}°$, where they turned west and sailed along the parallel of $15\frac{3}{4}°$ until December 16. So far they had come through an empty sea, and had seen no land of any description. Then the course was altered, and they ran west by north for 166 leagues, until they reached the latitude of $13\frac{3}{4}°$. After various changes of course, too many to record here, in the last day of the year they found themselves in latitude $6\frac{1}{4}°$—and yet no land. The crews and the subordinate pilots became uneasy, but Hernando Gallego was a stout-hearted man, having faith, and he writes in his journal :

" The pilots told me that I was the only person who was not disheartened after having sailed so many leagues without seeing land ; and when I told them that they would suffer no ill, and that, with the favour of God, they would see the land at the end of January, they all kept silent and made no reply."

Days and days they ran on, water failing, crews discontented and depressed, and the stout Gallego lying bravely as to his confidence of making land. " On this day (January 12, 1567) they signalled from the *Almiranta* (the General's ship) to ask where the land should be. I replied that it lay, in my opinion, 300 leagues away, and that, at all events, we should not sight it until the end of the month. At this time some of the people began to doubt whether we should ever all see the land. But I always told them that, if God was with them, it would be His pleasure that they should not suffer ill." A good man was Gallego, with no faint heart.

At length, on the 15th, they fell in with a little island, but, beating up to it on the following day, they found no safe anchorage. " Although being so near to this island, we could not get bottom with 200 fathoms." And so the Chief Pilot would not take the responsibility of remaining there. Whereat the soldiers murmured openly. " But," writes our sanguine chronicler, " I cheered them and consoled them with the assurance that they would meet with no misfortune, and that, with the grace of God, I would give them more land than they would be able to people." So they sailed on, and Gallego gave the little dangerous island the name of the Isle of Jesus. It has never yet been definitely determined which the island was.

On and on they sailed south-westward, until, on February 1, they sighted banks of reefs with some small islands in the midst. " We gave them the name of ' Los Bajos de la Candelaria,' because we saw them on Candlemas Eve." It is probable that these were the reef islands named by Tasman in 1643 " Ongtong Java," and which are otherwise known to-day as Lord Howe's Islands (do not confuse them with the little Lord Howe's Island between Australia and Norfolk Island). At last, on February 7, they reached the Solomons, and the first land they sighted of the group was the large island to-day known as "Ysabel." "This day," writes Gallego, "was Saturday, February 7, and the eightieth day since we set out from Callao, the port of the City of the Kings." It is worth while recording the first sight that the Solomon Islanders had of white men, in the language of one of the first white men to make their acquaintance, and the man whose courage and cheerful optimism was really responsible for the discovery of the group.

" Shortly after we arrived," says Gallego, " many large and small canoes came off to see us, displaying signs of amity. But they did not dare to come alongside the vessels ; and as we approached the land, they kept away. However, the General threw them some coloured caps, and being thus assured they came alongside the ships. The boat was launched, and in it went Juan Enriquez, with eight musketeers and target men (rodoleros) to see if they could find a port to anchor in, and also to search for the place whence the canoes had come. The rest of the natives became more con-

A VILLAGE IN THE SOLOMON ISLANDS

fident, and some of them came on board the ship. As they behaved well, we gave them things to eat and drink ; and they remained on board until it began to grow dark, when they got into their canoes and went ashore. And those who had gone away in the boat, seeing that it was getting dusk, returned without having found any port. As soon as it was dark we stood out to sea, and the natives in the canoes returned to their homes. They told us that for the sake of friendship we should have gone with them, and that they would have entertained us and given us plenty to eat."

So it will be seen that the Solomon Islanders' first impression of white men must have been an agreeable one. Alas ! it was not so long before it was altered.

## CHAPTER XI

### THE VOYAGE OF MENDANA (*continued*)

AFTER more trouble, Juan Enriquez found the harbour he had been sent in search of—not without having to be told by Mendana to " try again "—and the dauntless Gallego led the way through an opening in the surrounding coral reef in his ship the *Capitana*, the *Almiranta* following. " The harbour, which is in latitude of 7° 50″, we named the port of Santa Isabel del Estrella ; and we named the island Santa Isabel.

While Mendana occupied himself and his soldiers in the business of exploring the interior of the island—and, incidentally, in the burning of " many temples dedicated to the worship of snakes, toads, and other insects "—the indefatigable Gallego busied himself with the carpenters in felling trees and sawing planks for the building of a brigantine.

# The South Seas

The cutting of the timber was commenced on February 10, and she was launched on April 4. It can hardly be that in those days the Spanish vocabulary contained the word *manana* (to-morrow), which is so extensively used to-day. Busy as he is, Gallego finds time to record his impression of the natives. "These people," he writes, "are tawny and have crisp hair. They go naked, wearing only short aprons of palm-leaves. They have as food some moires or roots which they call *benaus*, and plenty of fish. They are, in my opinion, a clean race, and I am certain that they eat human flesh." The first evidence on which he supports the latter statement was furnished on March 15, when a fleet of fourteen canoes arrived, from another part of the coast, at the place where the brigantine was being built. The chief who was in command (Gallego calls him the *cacique*) sent the General, as a present, the quarter of a boy, including the arm and hand, together with some *benaus* (which we may call yams), inviting him to accept it as a token of goodwill. But, in order that the native mind might be disabused of any notions as to cannibalism being a Spanish practice, Mendana ordered the dainty morsel to be buried in their presence, which greatly abashed them, so that they returned whence they came.

When the brigantine was rigged and equipped, Mendana dispatched Gallego, with eighteen soldiers and twelve sailors, on a voyage of discovery. We cannot follow his cruise very minutely, but here is an extract from his journal which shows what kind of thorough seaman and navigator Gallego was. They had cruised along the coast of Ysabel, and had made a port where a trifling dispute with the *cacique* resulted in the latter's getting shot. "And as we sailed on, the mast sprung and nearly fell on us. Seeing what had happened, I ordered the sails to be secured and the tackle to be brought to the weather side, and in this manner the mast was 'stayed.' When the night overtook us we were without knowledge of any port, having much thick weather with wind and rain. Guided by the phosphorescence of the sea, we skirted the reefs ; and when I saw that the reefs did not make the sea phosphorescent, I weathered the point, and entered a good harbour at the fourth hour of the night, where, much to our ease, we passed [the remainder of] the night." When you come to consider this little feat, you will be as full of admiration for Gallego as is the author. As Dr. Guppy, his translator, remarks : " To find in a dark night and in thick weather an opening in a line of coral reef on an unknown coast is an undertaking fraught with the greatest hazard, even for a ship possessing steam-power. The only available guide is that which was followed by this clear-headed navigator ; but it is one which, as it depends on the luminosity of the sea, can only be of occasional service. When the sea has been unusually phosphorescent, each roller, as it breaks on the weather edge of the reef, is marked by a disconnected line of light, reminding one of the straggling fire of a line of musketry."

Gallego coasted along the south-east of Ysabel, and saw in the distance, across what is now the Indispensable Strait, the large island of Malaita, which he named the Isle of Ramos, because it was discovered on Palm Sunday (Domingo de Ramos). After various adventures with the natives— generally to the disadvantage of the latter—he made the south-eastern extremity of Ysabel, which he named Cape Pueto, on April 16. In the present chart it is called Prieto. From there he sails on to the island of Florida, passing, and recording in his journal, several islands. In Florida, which still bears the name he bestowed upon it, he was attacked in force, and with great determination, by the natives, whom he repulsed, killing many. Thence he sailed over to the volcanic island of Savo, which he named Sesarga, and which appears to have been at the time in a considerable state of activity. From Savo he crossed to the great island of Guadalcanar, which he reached on April 19. Here he had occasion to kill a few more natives. After a short stay and a little exploration, he started on the return voyage to Ysabel, going round the island, and rejoined Mendana about the end of April.

When the ship had been refitted they left the port of Santa Isabel de la Estrella, and proceeded to follow up Gallego's discoveries in the brigantine, and on May 12 were again at the port where Gallego had anchored in Guadalcanar. After a short rest—and more trouble with the natives—they sailed along the coast of Guadalcanar to the south-east. They then crossed over to the southern end of Malaita, and from there visited and explored the large island of San Cristoval. A good deal of time was spent in this part of the group, between San Cristoval and Guadalcanar. Finally, on August 11, they set sail from Puerto de la Visitacion de Nuestra Senora (these Spanish names are infinitely preferable to such as Bill's Lagoon), on the return voyage to Peru, which country they reached after many vicissitudes, and great hardships and dangers, in the first months of the year 1568.

Mendana's ships had spent six months in the Solomons—surely a most wonderous half-year of discovery and exploration. How those "Elizabethan" Melanesians regarded their visitors, or what opinion they formed of the White Man on a first acquaintance, we shall never know. All memory and tradition of the Spaniards has faded away in the centuries. But it could hardly have been a very favourable impression. From Gallego's journal—into which we have been able to dip only for the briefest moments—we find that the Spaniards' loss in men during their stay in the group did not exceed ten, whilst the natives must have lost at least ten times that number. Generally, it is true, the natives were the aggressors in the various conflicts which took place, but it was not always so, and the Spaniards seem to have displayed a lamentable callousness in the matters of kidnapping, and looting provisions and canoes. But if we are to pass judgment on Mendana and his men, we must recollect the spirit of the times in which they lived. Their zealous exploration was partly prompted by a desire to reclaim the infidel, and Spanish methods of so doing were not always of the gentlest or most conciliatory kind. We must remember, too, the situation in which the Spaniards found themselves—literally without a lease, and one which compelled them to "live upon the country," to exalt their prestige by any means, and to show nothing in their dealings with the savages by whom they were surrounded that the latter might regard as indicative of weakness. On the whole, whatever they may have done, we must be more greatly impressed by their daring and resource than by anything else concerning them. And of them all, no figure stands out so boldly, or shows so bravely, as that of the cool, clever, dauntless Hernando Gallego, Chief Pilot.

## CHAPTER XII

### THE WHITE MAN'S BURDEN

As we have seen in a previous chapter, whilst discussing the Dual Control of France and England in the New Hebrides, the Solomons—or, one should say, the British Solomons— have an advantage over their sister group in the fact that they are ruled by an undivided authority. Although both Germany and Great Britain divide the group unequally between them, each Power administers its own portion of it independently of the other. The two islands at the extreme western end—Buka and Bougainville, the latter the largest island in the Solomons—belong to Germany, whilst the remainder of the group is included in the British Protectorate.

# The South Seas

Formerly, both Choiseul and Ysabel were German also, but after the war in Samoa in 1899, and under the subsequent treaty between Germany, the United States of America, and Great Britain, these two islands were handed over to the last-named Power, in return for the cession of Samoa to Germany, with a coaling station in the latter reserved for America. It may be said at once that, beyond warning off British and other traders from the coasts of Bougainville and Buka, Germany makes small pretence—at present, at any rate—of administering or controlling her possessions in the Solomons.

The High Commissioner for the Western Pacific rules the whole of the British possessions in these seas from his head-quarters in Fiji, and he is, of course, responsible to the Colonial Office, and through it to the British Parliament. In the various groups Resident Commissioners administer local affairs, and are, in turn, responsible to the High Commissioner. In the New Hebrides, as we have seen, the British Commissioner works with a French Commissioner, and is responsible for the protection of British subjects and their interests in the islands to the High Commissioner in Fiji ; whilst the French Commissioner is answerable to his own authorities. Here in the Solomons the Resident Commissioner fulfils a similar function, but since authority over the whole Protectorate centres in himself, he is very much more of an absolute monarch than is his brother official in the New Hebrides. Within certain wide and well-defined limits, his word is Law in the islands, and he exercises an amount of power over a very large population such as is rarely seen nowadays in any part of the world.

If one wishes to behold an object-lesson in support of the British method of sustaining The White Man's Burden, he need go no farther than the Solomons to seek it. It is almost amazing to observe there what three or four white men of the right stamp can accomplish in the control, and the im-provement of condition, of hundreds of thousands of black

46

# The White Man's Burden

and savage people. Nowhere could there be a better example of the peculiar genius of the Englishman for the ruling of uncivilized subject races, and of his splendid natural capacity for reducing order and good government out of chaos and anarchy. Nowhere can there have been so much good work accomplished with such scanty means. It is a work which is carried on quietly and unostentatiously, almost out of sight of the world. Brief and modest Annual Reports—which are printed by the Colonial Office for the benefit of Parliament, given very small consideration by members of Lords and Commons, and not even read by any but an infinitesimal proportion of the public—are its only record. Newspapers know it not; the Man in the Street is wholly unaware of it. But it goes on—quietly, steadily, and surely—and some day the results of it will preach its soundness and its thoroughness. It is the peculiarity of such work, as carried on by the British, that it proceeds in its earlier stages without advertisement and without fuss, and it is not until long after the pioneers have disappeared from the scene that the completeness of their beginnings gains adequate recognition.

Consider the Solomons. The Commissioner has his headquarters at Tulagi in Florida, and maintains there the principal machinery of government in the shape of the bulk of his native police, and the very small amount of secretarial assistance with which he is provided. In the little Island of Gizo, in the western end of the Protectorate, there is another Government station. For the maintenance of these two stations, the keeping of order, the regulation of trade and customs, formerly for the control of the now abandoned Queensland labour traffic, the supervision of the traders, the protection of missionaries, the punishment of outrages, and the guarding of prisoners, not more than four white men and less than one hundred armed native police suffice, or, rather, are *made* to suffice. There is a Government yacht—a 70-tonner —with a white sailing-master and a native crew, and the police are armed with the old ·45 calibre Martini-Henry rifles. For grave occasions, such as the inflicting of exemplary punishment for serious outrages on the part of the natives, a man-o'-war is available, after a somewhat circuitous requisitioning through Fiji to the Admiral in Command of the Australian Station of the Navy. And there you have the tangible and physical means by which government, and good government, is maintained in the British Solomon Islands.

But it is very largely to moral rather than to physical forces that the good results obtained in the administration of the Solomons are due. The word " Protectorate " would seem to have been applied in its most literal sense, and the function of government to have been mainly understood in the light of that sense of the word. The native is made, firmly and unmistakably, to understand the meaning of the various " Thou-shalt-nots " which affect his existence. If he goes head-hunting the punishment meted out to him is swift, stern, and generally very certain. As a consequence, head-hunting is rapidly becoming a lost amusement. If he indulges in the pastime of missionary murder he suffers in life and property. Therefore missionary murder has lost much of its former popularity. If he slays his fellow-native, and is detected, the penalty he pays may be paid with his life. If he " cuts out " a trader's schooner or cutter, kills its owner and crew, and loots the vessel, terrible things happen to him. If he imports firearms, or is found in the possession of them, he is made a prisoner, and rewarded with a term of hard labour in the Government plantations, or on Government works of other sort. But woe betide the trader who maltreats the natives, either by using them harshly or unjustly, by seizing their property, or by shooting them down wantonly ! If his offence be proved, his punishment will be serious and severe, and of such a kind as is well calculated to deter other traders from mishandling the natives.

In this connection the author once witnessed an incident

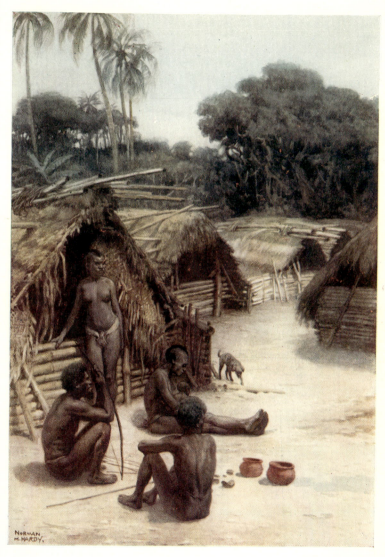

A VILLAGE IN THE NEW HEBRIDES

# The White Man's Burden

that impressed him deeply. Lying at anchor in a certain harbour of the Shortland Islands one hot afternoon, various of the officers and passengers of the trading steamer which visits the group every two months were amusing themselves by firing with a small-bore Winchester rifle at floating bottles and other marks thrown overboard from the ship. One of the engineers had the rifle in his hand, and about 300 yards distant a solitary native was paddling in a canoe across the glassy bay.

" See me scare that fellow," said the engineer. Suiting the action to the word, he put the rifle to his shoulder, and aimed at the water 50 yards in front of the advancing canoe. The bullet made a splash, and then, having ricochetted, another one about 100 yards beyond. It must have hummed directly over the man's head. Apparently it did not succeed in scaring him, for he continued on his course towards the ship. Unfortunately for the engineer, however, the Commissioner, who was also a passenger, happened to be walking up the deck behind him as he committed this rash and silly piece of folly. For ten minutes that engineer had about as bad a time as a man could have. The Commissioner rated him soundly, told him that his criminal foolishness might easily be the cause of another white man's losing his life, informed him that he had half a mind to give him—as lay in his power— three months' imprisonment off-hand, and there and then ordered the captain to send him to his cabin, whilst he (the Commissioner) considered the matter. It was a very scared and crestfallen engineer who descended precipitately to his cabin in the port alley-way.

It is this sense that he is likely to obtain justice, both in punishment and protection, that impresses the native. He will take advantage of the slightest indication of weakness on the part of his rulers, and will ever be ready to " take a slant " if he thinks one available. But he respects the strong hand, and when the strong hand is one that holds the scales of justice level, he speedily recognizes how his own interests lie.

# The South Seas

## CHAPTER XIII

### TRADE AND TRADERS

In the whole of Melanesia the staple and principal article of trade is copra. To all who know the South Seas the term is as familiar as the word " bread " ; but since every reader of this book may not have the good fortune to be acquainted with the South Pacific, perhaps some explanation will be necessary.

If you buy a coco-nut, and split it open, you will find it lined with a tough, white, more or less edible coating of from a quarter to half an inch in thickness. Well, that is copra, and its value lies in the oil which is extracted from it. The oil has innumerable uses, and a list of such everyday things as you are familiar with into which its composition enters would more than surprise you. A great deal of copra is collected in the bush by the natives, and bartered with the traders for " trade " goods of different description ; but of late years many plantations have been carefully cultivated in the islands, and the business of copra-growing has become almost as much a matter of farming as the growing of maize or wheat. Copra-growing, in the Solomons particularly (for the reason that that group is outside the sphere of the devastating hurricanes which sometimes afflict the Fiji Islands and the New Hebrides), is a very safe and extremely profitable pursuit. If you plant a plantation of, say, 30,000 young trees —which is the size of an average plantation—and can afford to wait the necessary five or six years for the trees to mature and begin bearing, you may reckon on each tree making you a return per annum of from one to two shillings, varying as the market price of copra fluctuates. Native labour is not expen-

# Trade and Traders

sive, and land is cheap, and it would seem that there are many harder ways of making money than by that of cultivating copra.

The method of preparing copra is as follows : When the coco-nuts have been gathered they are split in half, and the halves laid out to dry in the sun. Some traders dry them under cover in smoke-sheds, but the naturally dried copra is the best, and commands a slightly higher price than that which is dried artificially. After a little time the heat loosens the kernel of the nut, and when it has come away from the shell it is broken up into small pieces and spread out for a further drying process. When quite dry, it is put up in bags, and is then ready for export, and the further processes which the extraction of the oil entails.

Another product of the Islands is the ivory nut. This is the hard, heavy fruit of a palm of the same species as, and not unlike, the sago-palm, which grows wild in the bush. The nut itself has the shape of a small apple, is a dark brown colour externally, nearly as heavy as a billiard-ball, and hard and solid all through. The interior substance of it is white, and it is used very largely in commerce for making such articles as imitation ivory buttons, collar-studs, knife-handles, and a host of other things too numerous to mention. Its harvesting lies wholly in the hands of the natives, from whom the traders collect it in great quantities and at a price which varies with European demand, and a supply that is regulated by the vagaries of native industriousness. It is said that a tree only bears once, and then dies.

Pearls, pearl-shell, and bêche-de-mer are other articles of export. In the western end of the Solomons the pearl fisheries are rather extensive, though small as compared with those on the north and north-western coasts of the Australian continent. Bêche-de-mer is a horrible-looking sea-slug which is caught and dried for export to China, where the demand for it as an article of food is very great. Some white people like the soup made from it—and you may occasionally meet with it in the menus of Sydney or Melbourne restaurants—but the author must confess that to his taste, at any rate, it is suggestive of some by-product of a glue-factory.

Copra, however, is evil-smelling stuff, very rank and rancid in its odour ; ivory nuts are at their handsomest when made up into buttons or tooth-brushes ; pearl shell in the rough is not very pretty, and pearls are not for all of us ; bêche-de-mer is an abomination before the Lord. But a pleasing and a picturesque object is the South Sea Island trader who garners in these harvests of the palm-grove, the primeval forest, the clear opalescent lagoon, and the golden, sunlit beach. Him one may never tire of watching and wondering at. His story is a romance of tragedy and comedy ; his aspects are varied and fascinating ; his comings and his goings are the beginnings and the endings of adventure. He is of infinitely more interest to us than the things he collects with one hand, whilst he carries his life in the other.

There are many sorts and conditions of the trader, from the owner of Gavutu—whom we have seen in a previous chapter, master of potential wealth, Navy contracts, and little ships that scour the Islands in his interests—down to the lonely outcast dwelling by himself in the midst of fierce savages, upon their capricious sufferance. But in one respect or another they are all picturesquely interesting. And, another thing—they are all Captains. If a man is not a native, a Government official, a missionary, or a clerk of B.P.'s in Melanesia, you are quite safe in addressing him as " Captain." Occasionally it would be unsafe to neglect to do so.

Of course, such a trader, with such an establishment as we have briefly described at Gavutu, stands at the top of the tree. He comes next to the great companies, such as " B.P." With a large schooner, having an auxiliary oil-engine, in which he occasionally voyages to Brisbane or Sydney, he also runs many smaller craft, and has stations for the collection of produce

# Trade and Traders

scattered throughout the Islands. Next to him come the owners of such establishments as we have seen at Aola in Guadalcanar. They may possess a fairly large schooner, and cutter or two, and employ several white men in their navigation and the control of their storehouses. These men are their own masters—that is to say, if they are not too deep, financially, in the hands of the merchants from whom they obtain "trade goods" and supplies. But, in addition to them, there are the "captains" of the small craft that belong to the larger owners—hired men these, or perhaps having some arrangement as to commission on the amount of trade they bring in. Lastly, there are the solitary individuals settled in outlying islands who purchase copra and ivory nuts from the natives who surround them, and live hazardous, monotonous lives, only relieved by the visits of the little vessels that bring them "trade" and take away the results of their labours. It is not often nowadays that these individuals live entirely alone amongst the blacks. They generally have a white man as "mate." Very often they have married native wives, and have families of half-caste children.

It is these "smaller fry" that are most picturesquely interesting. They are a class of strong, hardy, self-reliant men, good fellows most of them, and usually kind and honest in their dealings with the natives. You will find scallywags and blackguards amongst them, of course, as amongst every class of man in the world, but it is quite safe to assert, without fear of contradiction from those who know them, that, with all their faults and vices, the South Sea Island traders are all round as fine a class of men, and as fine types of brave and vigorous manhood, as may be found anywhere. See one of them at the long steer-oar of his whale-boat, standing in his tanned bare feet, shooting through a narrow and dangerous opening in some surf-beaten coral reef; his cotton singlet, open at the neck, shows his sun-burnt chest; the mighty muscles ripple and swell about his broad back; the steadfast

53

eyes gaze ahead at the dangers he laughs over ; in his strong, resolute face there is the imprint of perils passed by land and water, the readiness to face whatever may be in store, the calm confidence of a strong man having confidence in his strength. He is the kind of man that makes you proud of manhood.

## CHAPTER XIV

### THE MISSIONARY

THE story of Mission work in the South Sea Islands is too long, and too full of detail, for proper consideration here. Its beginnings go back to the last years of the eighteenth century, and the story of the work and progress of the different societies and organizations which have laboured in the South Pacific—each according to its lights and doctrines, but all with the same object in view—is such a varied record of strenuous endeavour, courageous sacrifice, and the surmounting of terrible difficulties and discouragements, that two or three large volumes could hardly do it the justice which one small chapter of one small book could not possibly hope to do. It is too long a subject for us. All we can attempt is a peep at the missionary life. And, since it is to be a brief kind of peep, we will confine ourselves to one of the several organizations which labour in the Black Islands—the Melanesian Mission of the Church of England.

If you have never seen a missionary at work in his territory, the first aspect of one at his labours will be a little surprising to you. Most of us are fairly familiar with the external aspect at home of a bishop, a rector, or a curate. We know

# The Missionary

the bishop by his apron, his gaiters, and his peculiar style of top hat. The rector and the vicar and the curate we recognize by their sombre ecclesiastical clothing. We hear the bishop preaching in his cathedral, or addressing some public gathering ; we see the little maids in the villages curtsying to the parson as he goes his rounds, and the curate doing his good works in orthodox and regular style—but light suddenly on bishop or parson in the Solomon Islands, and it is very doubtful whether you will " spot " him for what he is for some little time. You may find him hanging on to a steer-oar in a whale-boat, or building a house—I have even seen one shinning up a coco-nut-tree.

One hot and breathless noontide a steamer on which the author was a passenger came into a harbour in the Solomons, and dropped her anchor. Boats came from the shore, and boats came from the sailing craft that lay close by, and soon the decks were full of pyjama-clad traders and natives. Now, though the trader is, on the whole, just such a fine, manly fellow as the last chapter described him, it is not at all unusual that he has a Past which has relegated him to the Islands, and the strenuous, dangerous life that is his. And often it has afforded the author some idle mental pastime—the vague and fanciful speculation as to what might have been the cause of the coming of this man or that man to these faraway seas. So, on this day he was leaning over the rail, under the shade of the awning aft, smoking, and indulging in various day-dreams as to the careers of the several white men who stood or sat about the deck of a little schooner that was being warped slowly alongside the steamer. That tall, good-looking man in the blue cotton shirt and old felt hat standing by the wheel, and giving orders in fluent pigeon-English to the native crew—that certainly was the captain. The red-faced, sturdy fellow forrard—he, no doubt, was the mate. It might have been drink that brought him here. One could not tell, of course, but it was interesting to make guesses to one-

self that were, afterwards, sometimes nearly right, and sometimes shockingly wide of the mark.  But the two who sat on
the combing of the hatch, and looked up at the high decks of
the steamer, occasionally waving a hand in cheery greeting to
someone they knew aboard—who might they be ?  One was
tall and muscular, with a broken nose set in a determined, bull-
dog, sun-tanned face.  The sleeves of his flannel shirt were
rolled up, and displayed muscular forearms.  He, without
doubt, was a prize-fighter, or had been one.  Of the other
it was not so easy to form an opinion.  He was clad in
soiled duck-trousers and a cotton shirt, and wore a battered
straw hat, and he, too, was muscular and brown and ener-
getic-looking ; but the Past that one might read from his
refined and handsome face was a little mystifying.  He did
not look as if he had had a very terrible or dissipated career.
It was difficult to account for his presence in the Islands.
One pieced together all sorts of imaginary histories to apply
to him.  One after another was rejected for a succeeding one
more fanciful and fantastic still.  At length, turning away as
the schooner was made fast, and he came running nimbly up
the ladder, followed by the pugilist, one said to oneself : " Ah,
poor beggar ! perhaps he made it no trumps when he should
have gone spades ; there is ' many a man driving a cab in
London to-day because he did not follow his partner's lead.' "
But one was wrong again.  Cards had not been his ruin, nor
drink, nor horse-racing, nor any other of the evil things that
sometimes bring people to the South Seas.  He was merely
the Bishop of Melanesia, and the broken-nosed " prize-
fighter " behind him was his acting-chaplain !

You will see from this little anecdote of a misconception
that missionaries in Melanesia are not disposed to allow the
niceties of clerical attire to interfere with their equipment
for the real hard work which is theirs.  It is pretty much the
same with members of the Wesleyan and Presbyterian Mis-
sions.  A dress suitable to the climate, and the exigencies of

CLIMBING AFTER GREEN COCO-NUTS     *Page 60*

# The Missionary

their calling, is the first consideration. The typical goat-bearded missionary of the scoffing comic paper—the alleged *pièce de résistance* of the cannibal menu—is a mythological personage who exists only in the brain of the comic person who draws him. The genuine article is usually an athletic type of vigorous manhood, capable of a good many physical accomplishments such as might easily be lacking in his cari-caturist.

The work of the missionary is hard, his recompense of success often scanty, and his failures and disappointments sometimes such as might break the stoutest hearts. In the past he has met with the greatest discouragement, and often the bitterest and most treacherous opposition, from other white men having to do with the natives. Disease and Death constantly menace him, and—though, perhaps, his is a happier lot amongst the savages of the South Seas than it would be amongst the savages of Whitechapel, Stepney, or Bethnal Green—he is called upon to face dangers and privations unarmed save with such moral arms as he has been equipped with by Nature. The quiet heroism of the Oxford or Cam-bridge man set down to do his work alone on the edge of some malarious jungle full of man-eating barbarians calls for as much praise and admiration as any of the brave deeds per-formed by soldier or sailor.

Apart from the fact whether one may appreciate a Chris-tianized native more than a heathen, or the reverse, the missionary has achieved one great and lasting good. He has secured " a fair deal " for the native. It is to his good in-fluence and splendid devotion that public opinion, both in the Islands and in the whole world, owes the generally healthy and fair-minded tone which animates it in its consideration of the treatment by white men of savage native races. Where he has succeeded in Christianizing communities he has enor-mously improved the physical as well as the moral being of his converts. Where he has failed—and he has often paid for temporary failure with his life—his own unselfish self-sacrifice has worked most often for ultimate good. John Williams, the great Bishop Selwyn, the martyred Patteson, "Tamate" Chalmers—their works live after them, as do those of the less noteworthy brothers who worked to the same noble end, and with the same fine purpose, as themselves. Hear how Robert Louis Stevenson—the fairest judge of man that ever was—sums them up, both the best of them and the worst: "With all their gross blots, with all their deficiency of candour, honour, and of common sense, the missionaries are the best and most useful whites in the Pacific." Whether one believes or not that Christianity is the right thing for the natives, one cannot but be full of admiration for the brave and devoted men who, believing that it is, have the courage of their belief, and the pluck and steadfastness to attempt its realization.

## CHAPTER XV

### ABOVE THE BEACH

Across the many-hued waters of the great lagoon the curving stretch of beach gleams against the dark green foliage of the jungly hill-side that towers above the coco-nuts, and sunlight—glaring hot sunlight—glows over all. No breath of stirring breeze ruffles the still surface of the wide-mouthed bay; the tufty tops of the palms are without the stir and rustle that the slightest zephyr sets them making. It is hot, and close, and quiet, the air full of that indescribable faint scent of the tropics, the warm moist atmosphere relaxing and enervating, and making for a kind of drowsy, listless laziness. Everything reflects heat. The glassy waters return it scorch-

# Above the Beach

ingly, the white bottom of the boat beats it back into one's face, bare boards, and seats, and thwarts are hot to the hand, and as we run up on to the dazzling beach upon which, so placid is the lagoon, hardly a ripple splashes, the glare from the white coral sands is almost blinding. Nothing but the dark shades of the mighty forest behind the palm-trees and the village relieve one's aching eyes. Above all is the deep, cloudless blue of an early forenoon sky.

Down come the men and children to meet us, walking slowly across the beach from the shelter of the palms, their black bodies as naked as Adam's—save for a little loin-cloth—the tubby children even lacking so much as that. Their musical laughter and jest sounds pleasant in the lazy morning, their smiles, and grins, and chucklings, as they help to run the dinghy up the beach, look like a cordial welcome—but maybe it is only impudent amusement. They lift our guns from the boat with roars of laughter, play with them (fortunately they are unloaded), aim at the palm-tops, at one another, at the ship lying out in the bay, fall down, pretending to be shot, and generally enjoy themselves, until Tomalo—our friend Tomalo—says something to them in their own language, whereat they become grave, some look a little scared, others mischievously amused, and the guns are politely handed to us.

Tomalo is the great man of the village—all the greater because he has been " alonga plantation longa Queenslan' one time "—and we go pigeon-shooting with him in the bush. A lithe, active fellow is Tomalo, supple and sinewy, dignified and graceful in his bearing, quick and springy in his walk. A little chubby, wondering-eyed, pot-bellied baby runs up to him as we walk towards the houses above the beach, and trots beside him, holding on to one tightly grasped finger, and twisting round from time to time to gaze at us. " This fellow he belong me," says Tomalo—" piccaninny belong me." Tomalo is proud of many things—of his travels to Australia, of his knowledge of " talky-talky," of his baby, of his manifest superiority to the " niggers," and proudest of all things in that he himself carries my gun.

The village smells with the sour smell of all native villages. Flies rise in clouds from little stagnant rain-pools, the pungent scent of wood-smoke drifts out of the dark doors of the grass houses, patches of yellow sunlight mottle the bare trodden earth in the open space between the dwellings, pigs walk about as if it all belonged to them, and scraggy fowls cluck and peck at the dirt. A little naked girl chases a strangely mongrel dog round a house with a stick. An old woman sits in a doorway smoking a short clay pipe, and shades her bleary eyes with a withered hand to gaze at us. A young woman, also smoking, hastily retires within doors as we approach, her thick ballet-skirt of dry grass rustling as she moves. " Tambak ?" whines the old woman, in a quavering voice, as we come near her—" Tam-bak ?" " She mother belong me—you got any 'bacca ? She savvy catch him," laughs Tomalo ; and we gain a toothless grin of appreciation from the venerable dowager at the price of a stick of black " trade " tobacco. Immediately our escort takes up the chorus, and we give away all we have brought with us. Even Tomalo junior, who is aged about five, produces his pipe, and lights up. We go to Tomalo's house at the end of the village, and the rest of the crowd hangs back respectfully at a distance. Tomalo calls to two youths, who immediately and miraculously climb two tall fruit-laden coco-nut-trees, and throw down half a dozen of the green nuts. Deftly they are husked and opened at one end, and we drink deep of the cool, refreshing, thirst-quenching " milk." " No good that fellow like rum," says Tomalo with a grin ; and we promise our friend that when he comes aboard next he shall have a drink of rum with us.

Tomalo's house is larger and better than the others of the village. He invites us inside, where, through the dim drift

60

of smoke from a little fire kindled in the midst, and in the
general obscurity of an interior that receives light only from
the low entrance, we see a young and comely woman nursing
an extremely young baby. " Mary belong me. Young fellow
mary, he belong me too." Tomalo introduces us to his wife
and youngest daughter. " Five mary belong me," he adds
proudly—" five mary—plenty piccanniny." " Blessed is he
who hath his quiver full," one compliments Tomalo, and the
happy man pretends to understand.

By-and-by we follow Tomalo into the bush, and in turn are
followed by the swarm of boys. Nearly all the women are
working in the gardens up the beach, and most of the men
are paddling round the ship in canoes, or going aboard her
with an eye to trade in curios.

It is wonderful in that great forest. Mighty trees support
a deep green roof, through which the sunlight filters in infre-
quent golden beams. Their huge, vine-clothed trunks rear
themselves up, like cathedral pillars, out of a dense and varied
undergrowth. Twisting vines, as thick as a man's arm, swing
from the spreading, rafter-like branches that support the roof.
Here and there a banana-tree or a graceful sago-palm catch
patches of sunshine on their beautiful fronds. Red hibiscus
flowers make bright patches of colour in the sombre green.
Ferns cluster at the foot of the trees. Delicate mosses clothe
their sides. Gay parrots, screaming and chattering, dart
through the high tree-tops. Now and again a native boy
points out a pigeon sitting up aloft, and we blaze away, and
sometimes get him, and sometimes don't. One, hit, sticks
in the fork of a tree. " Done, finish that one," says Tomalo,
and sends an active youth up to get the prey. When, after
a couple of hours spent in wandering along the native path-
ways, shooting often, giving Tomalo many shots—greatly to
his delight, and to the augmentation of his pride—and wholly
awed by the beauty and grandeur of the noble forest, we
return to the beach, we are followed by a train of bearers

with the " bag." Half we give to Tomalo, and half we take aboard. Tomalo comes with us in the dinghy, and he has *two* goes of rum when we reach the ship, so that he expands mightily, and talks with a pompous superiority of Pundaperg (Bundaberg in Queensland) and his doings there, and professes scorn and contempt for " niggers," and departs finally laden with cheap wooden pipes, " kaliko " (cheap print handkerchiefs), a huge butcher's knife, much trade tobacco, a smile like a gash in a pumpkin, and a hiccuppy enthusiasm for a second visit on the part of his friends. " You feller all same brother belong me," he exclaims fervently, as he wrings our hands at the gangway.

## CHAPTER XVI

### THE MELANESIAN AT HOME

THERE is a curious notion abroad amongst those who do not know him, or only know him superficially, that a coloured man living beyond the influence of the complicated thing we call civilization is " just nigger "—a living human being, it is true, but one that has little better regulation and order in his existence than a dumb animal. He is spoken of as " uncivilized." But that it is a wrong notion even the most rudimentary knowledge of the social arrangements and usages of nearly all savage races is convincing proof. Half a century ago the Japanese were considered to be " uncivilized." Have they changed their whole national nature in a short fifty years ? No ; the " civilization " was theirs for untold centuries ; they have merely adapted it to those conditions which they saw were inevitable if they were to continue as a people. Are the Melanesians " uncivilized " in the proper meaning of

# The Melanesian at Home

the word, which one takes to be, as applied to a race, the non-possession of rules and regulations and customs whereby the well-being of the community is safeguarded, rather than the caprice of the individual tolerated ? No ; in this sense they are distinctly " civilized "—more so innately, perhaps, than whole communities of low-class white people in England, America, or Europe. Barbarians, if you please, in the savagery of their habits and their disregard of bloodshed, but in the regulations that frame their morality they are generally more bound up than most Christians, and nearly as much so as Jews. They have their spiritual beliefs, their code of morals—and a strict code it is—their systems of finance, their laws as to life and property, their folk-lore, their mythological personages, their forms of worship, and their ways of accounting for their own existence and the general existence of life in the world. They may be wrong, according to our lights, but at any rate they have them. Life is more to them than a periodic empty stomach which has to be filled, or the mere exercise of the animal instincts which make for propagation. They are a long way from being " just nigger."

We have not yet discovered the origin of Life, the very earliest process by which it came into being. We have various pretty and fanciful ways of accounting for it, none of which are much more likely to be correct than that, for instance, of the people of Saa in the Solomons, who hold that men sprang spontaneously from a kind of sugar-cane which they call *tohu nunu*—when two knots in the cane began to shoot, and the cane below each shoot burst apart, and from one came out a man, and from the other a woman, to be the progenitors of mankind. That is but one of many of their theories as to creation. People who speculate as to their being are likely to have in them even the makings of the curious condition of evolution which we call " civilization," and for the want of which are too prone to despise and disregard simpler peoples.

# The South Seas

If we look at the social aspect of the Melanesians, the first striking thing that confronts us throughout nearly all the Islands that make up their country is their fundamental division of the people into two or more classes, which may not intermarry, and in which descent is counted through the mother. This is the first and main outlook of the Melanesian upon his fellows, and the whole base and foundation of Melanesian society. To quote the words of the Rev. Dr. Codrington, *the* authority in Melanesian anthropology: " There are no Tribes among the natives—if the word ' tribe ' is to be applied as it is to the Maori people of New Zealand, or as it is used in Fiji. No portion of territory, however small, can be said to belong to any one of these divisions ; no single family of natives can fail to consist of members of more than one division ; both divisions where there are two, and all the divisions where there are more than two, are intermixed in habitation and in property ; whatever political organization can be found can never be described as that of a tribe grouped round its hereditary or elective chief. It is probably true that in every account of Melanesian affairs given to the world tribes are spoken of, but a belief that every savage people is made up of tribes is part of the mental equipment of a civilized visitor. When one reads of the ' coast tribes ' or the ' bush tribes ' nothing more is meant than the people who inhabit the coast or the inland part of some island."

To go into all the rather complicated results of this basic element of Melanesian society is impossible here, but it is easy to grasp the main principle of it if we take a case where there are only two divisions or kins. Consider a man belonging to a division which, for convenience, we will term A. He must on no account take as wife an A woman. He must marry someone from the other division, which we will call B. Now, here comes in the Matriarchal system, the converse of our own social arrangement, which is Patriarchal —the children

IN THE DEPTHS OF A
MELANESIAN FOREST    *Page 61*

of the union will all belong to B. If we had any classification of the kind, they would naturally be A people, but in Melanesia it is just the reverse, and they inherit their B class through their mother. As a result, their mother's brother is considered to be a closer relation than their own father! It is to him that they look for that assistance in making a start in life which we naturally consider the duty of the father to provide. Were this system in vogue in England, it would not be the father whom the Crown would prosecute for neglecting his offspring, or failing to send them to school : it would be their maternal uncle. And, in the inheritance of property, a man's belongings do not go naturally to his own offspring, as with us ; they are passed on at his death to the children of his sister. If you consider this, you will quite easily understand why there can be no " Tribes " in the sense in which we almost invariably apply the word. There is, however, a question which will naturally occur to anyone in thinking over this curious and interesting social code. If a man *must* not marry any woman of his own division, but *may* marry any of the other, why should be not marry his own daughter, to whom he is not, as the Melanesians term it, *sogoi*—i.e., of the same kin ? But the marriage of those who are closely related, even though they are not *sogoi*, and may lawfully marry, is everywhere discountenanced. In the Island of Mota, as an instance, the children of a brother and sister, whom we should call cousins, are considered to be too closely related for matrimony. Brother and sister are A— their mother's division. The sister's children follow her, and are A also ; but the brother's are B, as was their mother. According to the law, an A person may wed with a B person ; but they will not do so. Such a match will never be made ; if it were, the parties to it would be said to " go wrong."

There is no rule, however, without an exception, and although this system generally holds good throughout all Melanesia, there are parts of the Solomons where there is no

# The South Seas

division of the people into kindreds, and where descent does, as with us, follow the father. In Ulawa, Ugi, and parts of the islands of Malaita, San Cristoval, and Guadalcanar, the Patriarchal system holds good. It is not known why this is so, but it is a fact that it is.

In a general way, to sum up, a Melanesian man regards all women—of his own generation, at least—as sisters and wives, and to a Melanesian woman men are all either brothers or husbands. Dr. Codrington quotes as an illustration of this the story of Taso, from Aurora in the New Hebrides, in which Qatu (a mythical personage) finds and brings to his wife twin boys, children of his dead sister. " His wife asks, ' Are these my children or my husband's ?' and Qatu answers, ' Your husband's, to be sure ; they are my sister's children.' In that island there are two divisions of the people ; Qatu and his wife could not be of the same—Qatu and his sister and her children must be of the same ; the boys, therefore, were possible husbands of Qatu's wife, but had they belonged to the other division their age would have made her count them her children rather than her brothers."

Altogether, to us it seems a strange and almost uncanny arrangement, but in any consideration of Melanesian life it is the one thing that must be held in view more constantly than any other. Here we have only attempted to outline and make it intelligible, but fuller study of it well repays those who take interest of more than a passing sort in things having to do with the multifold manifestation and the varying habits and customs of that strange beast, Man.

# The Melanesian at Home

## CHAPTER XVII

### THE MELANESIAN AT HOME (*continued*)

In the last chapter we have considered briefly the foundations and elements of Melanesian Society. This one we may commence with a brief account of the laws and usages regarding property, and the holding and passing on of it. Throughout Melanesia scarcely any difference exists in this regard. Succession, as we have seen, is with the children of the sister. This holds good universally, save where the succession of children may come into a case where the father has acquired property for himself. Property is in land and personal possessions, but there is some difference between land that has been inherited and land that has been reclaimed from the wild bush. There is, however, in a strict sense, no communal property in land.

With regard to the land, it may be taken that it is everywhere divided into three distinct sorts. There are the " Town lots "—the plots of ground on which the houses of individuals are erected in the villages ; the " Garden ground "—where the yams and bananas of each little settlement are diligently cultivated ; and the bush—which is simply the wild primeval forest and common hunting-ground. But the bush itself is hardly looked upon as property by the natives, nor do they assign any limits to the parts of it which might be taken to belong to the village or district in which they live, though there is no doubt that they resent interference with such parts of it as are adjacent to their cultivated grounds. The gardens, however, and the sites of the villages are held in portions as private property, and these portions can pass by inheritance. Every portion has its owner for the time being, who holds it as his share of the family property, but cannot sell it or give it away as if it belonged to himself alone. In a sale of land (which is a comparatively modern innovation due to the influence of Europeans) the consent of all who have an interest in the property must be obtained, and the exact limits of each plot defined. Then, every plot and every fruit-tree has to be valued, and the claim of every single individual discovered and satisfied. Curiously enough, a fruit-tree planted on another man's land, by his leave, remains the property of the planter and his successors. And it is also noteworthy that the divisions of property, in village or garden, do not correspond to the divisions of kindred for matrimonial purposes, but are all mixed up together, and held by families whose members must belong to different classes. No man's son is his own kin, yet father and son share the garden plot, and work it together.

In the succession to personal property—such as canoes, pigs, t ols, weapons, ornaments, etc.—there is a slight departure from the rule as to its being the right of the sister's children, but it is nevertheless very largely maintained as a right. A man's own kin may establish some claims, but for the most part, and in most of the islands, the sister's children are most likely to benefit by his death.

And now we come to the most difficult and complex aspect of the Melanesian—his attitude towards religion. Dr. Codrington says : " The religion of the Melanesians is the expression of their conception of the supernatural, and embraces a very wide range of beliefs and practices, the limits of which it would be very difficult to define. It is equally difficult to ascertain with precision what these beliefs are. The ideas of the natives are not clear upon many points ; they are not accustomed to present them in any systematic form among themselves." Every one who has had to do with native races is prepared to acknowledge that the longer he is amongst them, and the better he knows them, the more surely does he

# The Melanesian at Home

become convinced of his own ignorance of the native's mind, and of his processes of thought. A white man cannot think as a native thinks. A native is always reserved in his communication with white men. In nine cases out of ten, if a question be put to him, he will answer, not what he knows to be true, but what he fancies will be most acceptable to the white man. Go into a village and point to an image. " Debbil-debbil that one ?" you ask a native, and he promptly assents, knowing well that it is meant for nothing of the sort, but is probably a kind of symbol of some departed relative.

But, speaking very generally, if any definition as a whole can be given to the Melanesian's conception of the supernatural, and any name be found for his religion, or a religion foisted on to him, it might be stated as a sort of Ancestor Worship. Prayers and offerings are made everywhere to spirits and ghosts. The spirits of the dead are largely believed to have transferred their homes from men to beasts, birds, or fish. Sharks are, in many places, reverenced as being supposed to contain the spirits of the departed. But such worship only corresponds to our sense of religion.

Above all, the Melanesian believes in the existence of a supernatural influence called *mana*. *Mana* is a word and a meaning that carries through nearly all the islands and languages of the South Pacific. We cannot do better than by taking Dr. Codrington's definition of it. In a letter which Professor Max Müller quoted in the Hibbert Lectures of 1878, he writes : " The religion of the Melanesians consists, as far as belief goes, in the persuasion that there is a supernatural power about belonging to the regions of the unseen ; and, as far as practice goes, in the use of means of getting this power turned to their own benefit. The notion of a Supreme Being is altogether foreign to them, or, indeed, of any being occupying a very elevated place in their world. . . . There is a belief in a force altogether distinct from physical power, which acts in all kinds of ways for good and evil, and which it is of the

69

greatest advantage to possess or control. This is *Mana*. The word is common, I believe, to the whole Pacific, and people have tried very hard to describe what it is in different regions. I think I know what our people mean by it, and that meaning seems to me to cover all that I hear about it elsewhere. It is a power or influence, not physical, and in a way supernatural; but it shows itself in physical force, or in any kind of power or excellence which a man possesses. This *Mana* is not fixed in anything, and can be conveyed in almost anything; but spirits, whether disembodied souls or supernatural beings, have it and can impart it; and it essentially belongs to personal beings to originate it, though it may act through the medium of water, a stone, or a bone. All Melanesian religion consists, in fact, in getting this *Mana* for one's self, or getting it used for one's benefit—all religion, that is, as far as religious practices go, prayers and sacrifices." It will be seen from this that, even if we comprehensively class the Melanesian's religion as Ancestor Worship, we are a little beside the mark. What he is really desirous of is the use of his ancestor's *mana*. For the personal glory of the ancestral soul he hardly cares a fig of trade tobacco.

It is with the greatest regret that one is compelled to leave the consideration of this most intensely interesting and fascinating spiritual side of the Melanesian. But our space is too limited, and the end of our little book too imminent, to permit us to go into it very deeply. In the succeeding chapter, however, will be found some examples of his folk-lore, which may well serve to illustrate some phases of his mental processes. We have been able here only to indicate briefly the three most important aspects of his being. The strange and complicated system of the divisions of kin, his notions of political economy, and the broad outline of his religious convictions, are the things which count for most in his existence, and we have been able, at any rate, to note something, if only a little, concerning them.

# Fairy Tales

## CHAPTER XVIII

### FAIRY TALES

THE following stories, which have been translated from the Melanesian dialect by the Rev. Dr. Codrington, are very typical of the kind of fable in which the Melanesian delights. They are not by any means his best or most characteristic tales, but considerations as to space compel us to pass by some of the best and longer ones, in order to include an example from the Animal Stories, those concerning Myths and the origin of things, and the Wonder Tales. The value of these native stories is very great. They illustrate native life and the ideas which the native conceives of the world about him, and are interesting in a comparison with the folk-tales, not only of other savage peoples, but also with those of European origin. It is doubtful as to what extent the native takes them seriously, but there can be no question as to his belief in the existence of such supernatural beings as Qat. It is not likely that he really imagines birds and fish to be endowed with lingual capacities—he probably enjoys their talk much in the same way as we enjoy the conversations of Brer Fox and Brer Rabbit. The first tale comes from Ureparapara, in the Banks Islands.

*The Three Fish.*—" The story of the *Watwata* (an Ostracion) and the Sole. The two were scratching one another, and the Sole said to the Watwata, Scratch me. But the Watwata said, No, you shall scratch me first. And the Sole scratched the Watwata, scratched him well. And the Watwata said, Brother, you have scratched me badly, but the Sole said, No, it is all right. And the Watwata said, Well! now I shall scratch you in my turn. After that he scratched him,

71

scratched him extremely thin. And the Sole said, Well ! you have scratched me badly, but we two will play hide and seek. And the Sole said, You shall hide first. After that the Watwata hid, and got out of sight under a stone. The Sole sought him and found him. After that the Sole hid in his turn, and buried himself in the sand ; and the Watwata sought him in vain. But the *Song* (a fish which shows its teeth) stood and laughed at it ; and he has grinned so ever since. It is finished."

The next story comes from the Torres Islands, and belongs to those which have to do with myths and origins of people and things.

*The Mim.*—"They say that the Mim people dragged the yams from place to place, having brought them ashore at Hiw, and then dragged them to Tugua, for which reason the yams at Hiw and Tugua are very large and long. But when they dragged them along here to Lo, all the people were down on the reefs fishing and heard nothing of it ; nor did they know anything till they found the rind of the yams sticking to the roots of the trees along the path. These they picked up and planted ; and on that account the Lo yams are not very large, but plentiful enough. Because the Mim people sliced their yams in half for the men of Hiw and of Tugua, and then passed on to Toga, and sliced again for them there, on which account the yams there are very large and long. Afterwards they crossed to Ureparapara, where the people sliced the yams in half and planted them. They did the same in all the islands that way ; it was only at Lo that the people did not see and hear what was going on. The crowns of the yams remained and were planted somewhere. The Mim people went dragging the yams through all the islands, shouting and calling to the men of every place to come and slice the yams, and take their burden from them."

The third story is one of the Wonder Tales, and concerns the redoubtable Qat, or Qatu. Qat is a great figure in Melan-

72

PORTRAIT OF A SOLOMON ISLAND CANNIBAL     *Page 78*

# Fairy Tales

esian mythology—a good-humoured, rather benevolent spirit, with great *mana*, some impulses in the direction of mischievousness, and a taste for practical joking. In the Banl s Islands he has a very high reputation indeed. Even to-day, in those islands, a mother will reprove a naughty child or one crying for food with, " Do you think you are going to die ? Don't you know that Qat made you so ?" If a man drives a straying pig out of his house, he says to it, " Qat made you to stay outside !" He is credited with the regulation of the seasons, and his name is given to remarkable natural objects or effects. They speak of volcanic lava as his sauce ; a beam of light shining from a hole in the roof across a dusky house interior is his spear ; the flying shadow of a cloud over the sunlit sea is his shadow. But Qat is not a supreme being—he is " the hero of story-tellers, the ideal character of a good-natured people who profoundly believe in magic, and greatly admire adroitness and success in the use of it ; Qat himself is good-natured, only playfully mischievous, and thoroughly enjoys the exercise of his wonderful powers." It is sad that this story records the demise of Qat, but there are others that record the practical impossibility of " wiping him out." The following comes from Aurora, in the New Hebrides :

*The Winged Wife.*—" This is about the women that they say belonged to heaven, and had wings like birds ; and they came down to earth to bathe in the sea, and when they bathed they took off their wings. And as Qatu was going about, he chanced to see them ; and he took up one pair of wings and went back into the village and buried them at the foot of the main pillar of his house. Then he went back again and watched them. And when they had finished bathing they went and took up their wings and flew up to heaven ; but one could not fly because Qat had stolen her wings, and she was crying. So Qat goes up to her, and speaks deceitfully to her, and asks her, What are you crying for ? And she says, They have taken away my wings. Then he takes her to his

s.s.          73          10

house and marries her. And Qat's mother takes her, and
they go to work; and when the leaf of a yam touches her
there are yams as if someone had already dug them up, and
if a leaf of a banana again had touched her, just a single one,
all the bananas were ripe at once. But when Qat's mother saw
that things were so she scolded her; but not Qat; he was gone
shooting birds. And when Qat's mother scolded her she went
back into the village; and she sits beside the post of the house
and cries. And as she cried her tears flowed down upon the
ground and made a deep hole; and the tears drop down and
strike upon her wings, and she scratches away the earth and
finds them, and flies back again to heaven. And when Qat
was come home from shooting he sees that she is not there,
and scolds his mother. Then he kills every one of his pigs,
and fastens points to very many arrows, and climbs up on the
top of his house, and shoots up to the sky. And when he sees
that the arrow does not fall back he shoots again and hits the
first arrow. And he shoots many times, and always hits, and
the arrows reach down to the earth. And, behold, there is
a banyan root following the arrows, and Qat takes a basket of
pig's flesh in his hand and climbs up to heaven to seek his wife.
And he finds a person hoeing; and he finds his wife and takes
her back; and he says to the person who is hoeing, When
you see a banyan root don't disturb it. But as the two went
down by the banyan root and had not yet reached the ground,
that person chopped the root off, and Qat fell down and was
killed, and the woman flew back to heaven. That is the end
of it."

It would be interesting to know whether this is an old story,
handed down for many generations, or whether it has been
invented since the coming of the missionaries. The winged
woman from heaven is not a little suggestive of an angel.

# The Warpath

## CHAPTER XIX

### THE WARPATH

ALTHOUGH there are many aspects of the life of the Melanesian which we have perforce been unable to afford space for, it would hardly do to leave him without taking some notice of those of a warlike character. It may be said at once that the principle which animates a Melanesian warrior on the war-path is that which is the guiding light of the South African Boer when he goes forth to battle. His great object is to kill the enemy without getting killed himself, and the latter consideration is, perhaps, the more important of the two. In the case of the Melanesian, his mode of warfare has been stigmatized as cowardly, but who would call the Boer a coward now? It is true that very often an expedition to attack a neighbouring village, on the part of a community of Melan-esians, turns out to be nothing more nor less than a cunningly organized and executed murder plot; but that he can fight bravely and sustainedly on occasion, and even against heavy odds, has been proved on more than one bloody little island battle-field. He never shows up so well as a fighting man as when he has been suddenly attacked and compelled to give battle, but he is sometimes not wanting in the capacity for sustained and difficult offensive operations. The daring attack on Gallego in the Island of Florida is a case in point. "When the Indians," he writes in his journal, "saw that we were about to shift our position, they got into their canoes in a great hurry, with their bows and arrows, and clubs, and many stones; and in a very fierce manner they began to shoot their arrows and stones at us. Seeing their daring, we replied with the muskets, and many Indians were killed, and the whole were repulsed ; and they rallied and came on to the attack with greater fury ; but this time they suffered even more, and for the second time they were repulsed and routed." That they should have made so persistent an onslaught upon men the like of whom they had never seen before, whom they believed to be of another world than their own, and who possessed terrible death-dealing weapons of which they had no previous know-ledge, bespeaks for them the possession of an amount of courage of no mean degree.

The use of the bow is almost universal throughout Melanesia, but it is not everywhere the principal weapon employed in warfare. In some islands—as Florida, Guadalcanar, Ysabel, San Cristoval, and parts of Malaita—the spear takes precedence of it. As a protection against the thrown spear, shields are largely used, but in San Cristoval a long, curved glaive takes its place. The spears are usually made of palm-wood, and are mostly barbed in a fashion that makes one shudder to think of the kind of wound they must inflict when driven fairly " home." In Florida they are tipped with human thigh-bones, cut into horrible jagged points. Fighting in the open, however, is not usually attended by a heavy casualty list. It is when an unsuspecting village is ambushed, or a small party waylaid in the jungle, that the greatest execution is done. Slings are occasionally employed here and there, and are said to have first come into use as a means of attacking tree-houses. Clubs—the first natural weapon to man after his hands—are universal. For any reader to whom the British Museum is available, there is opportunity of studying a splendid collection of Melanesian weapons in the Ethnological Gallery. Not long ago, in a very old and picturesque inn in a North of England town, the author came across a miscel-laneous collection of Solomon Island weapons and canoe-paddles, evidently very old, and of which no one about the place knew the history, or even whence they might have come. It was strange to see these relics from the far-away South

# The Warpath

Seas in that old hostelry dating back to early Tudor times. Strange—and a little disquieting, for they revived a certain restless hankering after reef and palm, beach and lagoon, blue seas and soft warm tropic airs, that ever besets any who have been in the Islands.

But the weapon of the Melanesian to which most interest attaches is the poisoned arrow. In a collection you may recognize them generally from their appearance. They are long, thin reed-shafts, with a hardwood foreshaft tipped with six or seven inches of human bone, which is smeared with a dark substance. If the tips are provided with little guards, you may be quite certain that they are the genuine article, and would do well to handle the sharp points with extreme care.

Amongst traders and occasional visitors to the Black Islands, it is generally believed that the natives' arrows in certain parts of the different groups really are poisoned, in the sense in which we use the word, and the same belief prevails generally throughout Australia. But such is not really the case. Careful and independent medical examination has established the fact that the supposedly poisonous matter with which the arrow-heads are smeared is not so, and that whatever fatal effects may result from wounds inflicted by them are due, not to poison, but either to the nature of the wound itself, or to *tetanus* (lock-jaw) arising from the employment of the bone hasp, climatic, septic, or other reasons. They are to the native mind certainly very "poisonous," but for quite another reason. It is again a question of *mana*. What they think of, when making their arrows, and what they firmly believe to be obtained, is a weapon endowed with supernatural power by the material from which it is made, and qualities added by charms and magical preparations. "The point is of a dead man's bone, and has therefore *mana*; it has been tied on with powerful *mana* charms. That is what they mean by what we, not they, call poisoned arrows. And when the wound has been given, its fatal effect is to be aided and carried on by the same magic that has given supernatural power to the weapon." The so-called " poisoned " arrows are used in the Solomons, Santa Cruz, the Banks Islands, and the New Hebrides.

Thanks to the vigilance and energy of the Government, head-hunting in the Solomons has greatly decreased of late years ; but it is still occasionally indulged in, either as a cause for, or an accessory to, warfare. But even in its palmiest days this pleasant hobby was more or less confined to the western end of the group, and was not practised by natives living in islands to the eastward of Ysabel. The western natives, however, made long raids to the east in expeditions that lasted for months, and inflicted severe losses on the coasts of Malaita, Guadalcanar, and Florida, returning home with great numbers of their ghastly trophies. The rest of the Solomons confined themselves to merely taking heads and preserving them when they came their way—as those of enemies killed in battle, or of sacrificial victims. They did not organize collecting expeditions. The gentle sport of the head-hunter has been greatly discouraged by various commanders of men-o'-war whilst in the group, and it is interesting to record that the name of Captain (now Rear-Admiral) Davis—then of H.M.S. *Royalist*—is still, some fourteen or fifteen years after, remembered with awe, on account of the salutary lessons he taught certain of the more prominent head-hunting chiefs and communities.

Cannibalism still undoubtedly exists in various parts of the Solomons and New Hebrides, though there has never been any in the Banks Islands and Santa Cruz. But it is a popular misconception that the practice of cannibalism is generally pursued for dietary reasons. " To kill for the purpose of eating human flesh, though not unknown, is rare, and is a thing which marks the man who has done it." The bodies of foes slain in battle are eaten in many parts of Melanesia, but not by way of rations. The universal *mana* is again to be taken into consideration, for the conqueror adds the prestige and courage of the man slain to his own stock by consuming some portion of his remains. In certain sacrificial feasts, also, cannibalism plays its part. But it may be taken as a general thing that it is rather ceremonial than practical. The victim of a feast has more connection with *mana* than with meat.

## CHAPTER XX

### GRACIOSA BAY

DAWN—and the glow of yellow and orange and crimson stealing up into the sky to eastward across the Bay. Towering masses of billowy cumulus clouds lift above the tree-tops on the summits of the dark forest-clad hills upon the opposite shore, and turn slowly from a pure white, that stands out against the cold indigo of the departing night, to a faint glow of pink that as slowly merges into deeper rosy light. The wide waters take the colour, too, in their calm, motionless, rippleless, looking-glass surface, and change from a deep, cold green to opal tints and lights. Hill and jungle and rocky point paint themselves in the waters as the light grows stronger. The calls of birds float across from the bush. The first rays of the unrisen sun gild the tree-tops against the glowing clouds, the gilding creeps down the far hill-sides, and suddenly, startlingly suddenly, the red disc of the sun appears over the dark jungle above the Bay. The oily waters glint and sparkle with dazzling, wavering, serpentine streaks of light. The trees along the shore stand out against the sombre depths of the forest behind them. Overhead, the sky assumes its deep sapphire, daytime tint. The beach below the village turns to a glowing whiteness. A spiral of blue smoke twists thinly up against the deep green of the hills. A cock crows, and the flapping of his wings comes clearly over the water. A single canoe with a solitary native in it glides out towards the ship. Santa Cruz is awake.

Little, faint whiffs of thin mist begin to waver above the Bay. It is warm and close. Breathlessly the day matures, and rapidly grows hotter as the sun ascends. One rolls lazily off one's grass sleeping-mat upon the poop, gathers pipes and tobacco and matches from the deck, and makes the early-morning pilgrimage forrard to the galley in search of coffee. Other sleepy-eyed, rather tired apparitions—it is hard to sleep soundly, even on deck, in these warm nights—gather by the galley doorway, and yawningly demand refreshment, which having obtained and consumed, they make the morning fragrant with tobacco, as they betake themselves to duty, or to loafing over the port rail, and gazing at the shore, and spitting in the water, and remarking on the peculiar odour of the natives as they begin to swarm out to the ship in their little outriggers. For the Santa Cruz people do indeed smell bad. It is a sour, offensive, depressing smell, something like a holdful of copra—only worse—and as it wafts about the ship all day, it makes you wish to throw every nose-ringed, naked nigger overboard, and get to sea for purification and disinfection. Their effective range is quite 300 yards.

It is a beautiful Bay—a Bay of a thousand delights. But its people are not beautiful, and their personal decorations add to their ugliness. They are short, sturdy fellows, daring and expert thieves, utterly unimpressed by the white man's *mana*, always fully armed with bows and arrows—and they will face a rifle with them, too—keen to trade, but sharp as a Petticoat Lane gutter merchant. They have often a Jewish cast of countenance, and from a rather Hebraic nose depends

HEAD HUNTERS SETTING OUT ON A RAID    *Page 78*

# Graciosa Bay

a flat disc that hangs over the mouth, and gives them an inexpressibly hideous appearance. Some wear a peculiar kind of grass-made stove-pipe hat without a crown, others have discs of white *tridacna* shell, ornamented with tortoise-shell fretwork of frigate-birds and other designs, fixed to their foreheads. All are as nearly naked as possible, and the smell of them is an abomination.

Down on a cleared point towards the harbour's mouth, and on the eastern shore, is the house of the only trader in Santa Cruz. His white schooner is anchored off the point. He and his mate live there alone, and by sheer force of character maintain a footing amongst those savage, fearless people. Sometimes, in one way or another, he contrives to offend them —they are very susceptible to offence ; then they attack him. But it is a curious business, for they always punctiliously send him word of the day and hour they mean to come. He barricades his dwelling and store, arms his " boys "—who, as is the case always, are recruited from other islands in order to guarantee their loyalty—and makes ready for the fray. At the hour appointed the natives rush out of the bush, fire a few flights of arrows, which stick harmlessly into the wooden walls of the house, and receive in turn several rifle volleys, purposely aimed over their heads. Their " honour is satisfied," friendly relations are re-established, and trade resumed. But it is said that they will kill him some day. Perhaps they have done so by now, but one hopes not. He was a good fellow.

Here ended, 300 years ago—in this same lovely Bay— Spain's dreams of conquest in the Southern Seas. It is a pathetic story. Twenty-five years after his voyage of discovery to the " Isles of Salamon," Mendana—still under that strange Island spell that calls men back—sailed again from Peru, with four ships and 400 people, to colonize the Solomons. Their destination was San Cristoval, but they never found it, and one dark, wet night they came to Santa Cruz. That same night disappeared from the ken of white men one of the ships—the *Almiranta*—and from then until to-day no trace of her has ever been discovered. Whither she went or what fate overtook her is one of the many mysteries of the sea. Despairing of finding San Cristoval, Mendana planted his colony here at Graciosa Bay. And then followed a hurricane of disaster for the little settlement. Disease and the natives' arrows killed many. Mutiny broke out. Mendana died broken-hearted, and, to the superstitious Spaniards, an eclipse of the moon which preceded his death must have seemed like the wrath of Heaven directed against their enterprise. His successor in command was killed by the natives two weeks after, and in a little over two months from the time of their arrival the survivors resolved to abandon Santa Cruz. Hoping to obtain tidings of the missing *Almiranta*, Quiros, who was chief pilot, sailed westward, but on the second day they gave up the search, and headed for Manilla. Had they continued on the same course for a few hours longer, they would have sighted San Cristoval, and the Solomons would have been rediscovered for Spain. But they were lost, and never found again for 150 years. Two only of the ships reached the Philippines. The *Fragata* never appeared again. It was afterwards reported that she had been found ashore with all her sails set, and all her people dead.

There is no trace of the Spaniards at Graciosa. There is no tradition of them amongst the natives. Their graves have been lost in the centuries. Time has obliterated all their footsteps. One thing one would like, romantically, to establish as a record of them—but it must, sadly, be numbered amongst the improbabilities. Alone of all the islands in Melanesia, Santa Cruz has in use the European loom for the weaving of their beautiful mats. One wonders—but is assured that there is no hope for the pleasing fancy.

And so here, where the Spaniards departed from Melanesia, we too will take our departure; and if we leave these splendid islands with regret, at any rate our port of departure is a beautiful one, and our last night of the Black Islands something to remember always. So out we sail from the wide Bay to the blue waters of the open sea, and the blue cone of the volcano Tinakula lifts for us on the horizon's edge as we leave the Black Islands.

**THE END.**

BILLING AND SONS, LIMITED, PRINTERS, GUILDFORD

OTHER BOOKS
FOR
BOYS & GIRLS

ILLUSTRATED
IN COLOUR
LIKE THE

PEEPS AT MANY
LANDS

I

# THE WAVERLEY NOVELS

## By SIR WALTER SCOTT

THE Authentic Editions of Scott are published solely by A. and C. BLACK, who purchased along with the copyright the interleaved set of the Waverley Novels, in which Sir Walter Scott noted corrections and improvements almost to the day of his death. The under-noted editions have been collated word for word with this set, and many inaccuracies, some of them ludicrous, corrected.

## LIST OF THE NOVELS

Waverley
Guy Mannering
The Antiquary
Rob Roy
Old Mortality
Montrose, and Black Dwarf
The Heart of Midlothian
The Bride of Lammermoor
Ivanhoe
The Monastery
The Abbot
Kenilworth
The Pirate

The Fortunes of Nigel
Peveril of the Peak
Quentin Durward
St. Ronan's Well
Redgauntlet
The Betrothed, etc.
The Talisman
Woodstock
The Fair Maid of Perth
Anne of Geierstein
Count Robert of Paris
The Surgeon's Daughter, etc.

| | | |
|---|---|---|
| **NEW POPULAR EDITION** 25 volumes | Demy 8vo. Illustrated paper covers, with at least two woodcuts in each vol. | Paper, **6d.** Cloth, **1/-** |
| **VICTORIA EDITION** 25 volumes | Crown 8vo., bound in cloth, and Illustrated with frontispieces | **1/6** per vol. |
| **TWO SHILLING EDITION** 25 volumes | Crown 8vo., green cloth. Illustrated with woodcut frontispieces and vignettes | **2/-** per vol. |
| **STANDARD EDITION** 25 volumes | Crown 8vo., red art canvas. Illustrated with 25 photogravure frontispieces | **2/6** per vol. |
| **DRYBURGH EDITION** 25 volumes | Large crown 8vo., green cloth, gilt top. Illustrated with 250 page woodcuts | **3/6** per vol. |
| **CENTENARY EDITION** 25 volumes | Crown 8vo., red cloth. Illustrated with 150 steel plates | **3/6** per vol. |

A. AND C. BLACK . SOHO SQUARE . LONDON, W.

# SCHOOL AND COLLEGE TALES

## By F. W. FARRAR.

---

**Eric :** or, Little by Little. A Tale of Roslyn School. Containing 8 full-page Illustrations in colour by G. D. Rowlandson, and 78 in black and white by Gordon Browne. Large crown 8vo., cloth, price **3s. 6d.**
　　Containing 78 Illustrations by Gordon Browne. Large crown 8vo., cloth, price **2s. 6d.**
　　Containing Frontispiece and coloured Illustration on cover. Crown 8vo., cloth, price **1s. 6d.**
　　Crown 8vo., cloth, ink design and lettering, price **1s.**
　　* Demy 8vo., with picture design in colour on paper covers, price **6d.**

**St. Winifred's :** or, The World of School. Containing 8 full-page Illustrations in colour by Dudley Tennant, and 152 in black and white by Gordon Browne. Large crown 8vo., cloth, price **3s. 6d.**
　　Containing 152 Illustrations by Gordon Browne. Large crown 8vo., cloth, price **2s. 6d.**
　　Containing Frontispiece and coloured Illustration on cover. Crown 8vo., cloth, price **1s. 6d.**
　　Crown 8vo., cloth, ink design and lettering, price **1s.**
　　* Demy 8vo., with picture design in colour on paper covers, price **6d**

**Julian Home :** or, A Tale of College Life. Containing 8 full-page Illustrations in colour by Patten Wilson, and 10 full-page Illustrations in black and white by Stanley Berkeley. Large crown 8vo., cloth, price **3s. 6d.**
　　Containing 10 full-page Illustrations in black and white by Stanley Berkeley. Large crown 8vo., cloth, price **2s. 6d.**
　　Containing Frontispiece and coloured Illustration on cover. Crown 8vo., cloth, price **1s. 6d.**
　　Crown 8vo., cloth, ink design and lettering, price **1s.**
　　* Demy 8vo., with picture design in colour on paper covers, price **6d.**

　　* The above are also bound together, in cloth, price **2s. 6d.**
　　Or ERIC and ST. WINIFRED's together, cloth, price **2s.**

---

PUBLISHED BY A. AND C. BLACK . SOHO SQUARE . LONDON, W.

3

# ANIMAL AUTOBIOGRAPHIES

EDITED BY

## G. E. MITTON

EACH CONTAINING 12 FULL-PAGE ILLUSTRATIONS
IN COLOUR

SQUARE CROWN 8VO., CLOTH, GILT TOP

PRICE **6/=** EACH

The *Observer* says: "That a great many children, and their elders, too, take a continuous interest in the life-stories of animals has been proved again and again, and therefore the idea of this series is one which is sure to commend itself to a large circle of readers. These volumes show that the happy idea has been very happily carried out."

PUBLISHED BY

A. & C. BLACK, 4, 5, & 6, SOHO SQUARE, LONDON, W.